PHARAOHS

THE RULERS OF ANCIENT EGYPT FOR OVER 3000 YEARS

PHARAOHS

THE RULERS OF ANCIENT EGYPT FOR OVER 3000 YEARS

PHYLLIS G. JESTICE

amber
BOOKS

First published in 2023

Published by
Amber Books Ltd
United House
North Road
London N7 9DP
United Kingdom
www.amberbooks.co.uk
Instagram: amberbooksltd
Facebook: amberbooks
Pinterest: amberbooksltd

Editor: Michael Spilling
Designer: Andrew Easton
Picture researcher: Terry Forshaw

ISBN: 978-1-83886-316-6

Printed in China

CONTENTS

INTRODUCTION: THE AGE OF PHARAOHS

For more than 3,000 years, ancient Egypt was ruled and shaped by its kings. About 170 of these monarchs are known today. They were mostly men but count a few women in their ranks. The majority were native Egyptians, but sometimes foreign dynasties took the throne and with it the ceremonial traditions that surrounded the person of 'pharaoh' – a term that means 'the palace' but gradually came to refer to the monarch.

OPPOSITE: In life, pharaohs were avatars of Horus, but upon death were regarded as a form of the god Osiris, first king of Egypt and god of the dead. This Twentieth Dynasty relief from Thebes depicts Osiris holding the crook and flail of kingship.

RIGHT: A gold bracelet from the tomb of Amenemope, Twenty-first Dynasty (Tanis 993–984 BC). On the rear are cartouches bearing the royal names of the king's predecessor Psusennes I. Amenemope's tomb is notable for being one of only two entirely intact royal burials.

ABOVE: **The Tutankhamun exhibition in Bratislava, Slovakia, on 14 December 2014. The designers of this international tour caught well the appearance of the tomb when it was first opened and the jumble of objects that confronted Howard Carter and Lord Carnarvon.**

Whether Egyptian or outlander, whether male or female, all were able to tap into the great resources and wealth of Egypt to an extraordinary degree, leaving behind monuments and tomb treasures (those not pilfered by ancient grave robbers) that still inspire awe today. Perhaps no rulers in world history have been so much the personification and focal point of their state, or have controlled the resources of their land as much as the pharaohs did.

But what were these pharaohs? Were they unrestrained despots who forced their subjects to serve them and let their people starve while they themselves were buried with tonnes of gold? Or did their subjects gladly perform the labour that created pyramids, temples and tombs, believing that their service promoted the right order of things and assured their own prosperity and blissful afterlife? The truth of the matter was certainly somewhere between these two extremes. As we will see, some of Egypt's kings did have a reputation for harshness in their own lifetimes, but others were renowned for their kindness and sense of justice. Similarly, while some of the compulsory labour that constructed edifices such as the pyramids was likely voluntary – workers were provided with food and most of the work would have been done at times when the Nile's annual inundation made farming impossible – others resented it, as can be seen from the draconian punishments meted out to shirkers.

It is all too easy to regard the history of the Egyptian monarchy as a monolith, an institution stubbornly unchanging and unchangeable even as the world beyond Egypt's borders was transformed. While the ideology of kingship was remarkably conservative, however, pharaohs over time naturally responded to both internal and external change. After all, pharaonic Egypt spans an immense period, from the unification of Egypt sometime around 3000 BC to the death of the last rulers of an independent Egypt, Cleopatra VII and her son Ptolemy XV (Caesarion), in 30 BC. Ancient authors already recognized that pharaohs did not all share a common bloodline, dividing Egypt's history into 30 'dynasties' (and acknowledging that sometimes even the members of the same dynasty were not related to each other). In the 19th century, scholars marked broad changes in Egyptian society by dividing ancient Egyptian history into Old, Middle and New Kingdoms, with 'intermediate' periods of disunification between them. We now also recognize a Third Intermediate Period, Late Period and Ptolemaic period. This book will for the most part follow those traditional divides, and uses the chronology favoured by *The Oxford History of Ancient Egypt*, edited by Ian Shaw.

ABOVE: The English Egyptologist Howard Carter (1873–1939) examining King Tutankhamun's inner coffin with an unnamed Egyptian assistant, shortly after the discovery of Tutankhamun's tomb on 4 November, 1922.

DECODING ANCIENT EGYPT

Despite the efforts of archaeologists, historians, philologists and even forensic scientists for nearly two centuries, there are still many gaps in what we know about the rulers of ancient Egypt. Some are known only by name. For others,

HOW WE KNOW

The Egyptians themselves preserved the memory of their kings for thousands of years. We have several 'king lists' – names of rulers in chronological order, sometimes with notes about significant events of their reigns. The oldest is the Palermo Stone, part of a Fifth Dynasty basalt stela carved in *c.*2400 BC. Piecing together its fragments, now spread among several museums (the largest in the Palermo Archeological Museum), it tells of a mythic past when the gods ruled directly, eventually passing the throne to a human, and carries the list up to the time it was carved. The two other most important king lists are the Turin Canon and Manetho's history of Egypt, the *Aegyptiaca*. The Turin Canon is a papyrus, written in hieratic, compiled in the reign of Rameses II. Regarded as the most reliable king list, it was badly damaged

when it was shipped to Turin, and some of the names cannot be deciphered. The much later Egyptian scribe Manetho used these sources or other temple king lists when he wrote his major history of dynastic Egypt in the 3rd century BC. Unfortunately, Manetho's work too only exists in a fragmentary state, largely in the form of long extracts quoted by later Greek and Roman writers. The loss is particularly regrettable, because Manetho had access to priestly archives, as did the Greek Herodotus, who devoted a whole book of his *Histories* to Egypt.

BELOW: **Dr Myriam Krutzsch, papyrus restorer of the Egyptian Museum in Berlin, checks the position of fragments of the Turin King List. Her work and that of other papyrologists has played a vital role in reconstructing the history of ancient Egypt.**

a tomb, sometimes staggeringly impressive, is the sole clue to the role they held in life. With every archaeological dig, the possibility exists that a new piece will be added to the puzzle. But without a doubt, the most important advance in our knowledge came with Jean-François Champollion's decipherment of hieroglyphs, the ancient Egyptian writing system, in the 1820s. Surviving literature, accounts, even trial transcripts that survived on fragile papyrus thanks to the desert conditions of Upper Egypt started bringing this long-dead era to life. The walls of temples and tombs added immensely to our understanding of pharaohs and other important people, thanks to the millennia-long habit of inscribing boastful autobiographies on any available flat surface. Such accounts need to be read with a critical eye, but are extremely valuable relics of the past.

ABOVE: **Sir Flinders Petrie (1853–1942) and his wife Hilda Urlin excavated many of Egypt's most important archaeological sites, setting a new standard for archaeology with his careful and painstaking methods. He developed a system for determining the age of a site based on the styles of pottery found.**

MORE THAN MERE MORTALS

Again and again, such wall carvings show us pharaoh, larger than mere mortals, equal in size and able to stand face to face with the great gods of Egypt. Statues, sometimes massive, help drive home the message that the kings of Egypt were more than mere mortals. They were in fact gods, or at least semi-deities in the process of reaching full divine status.

Pharaoh's godhood was a key concept of royal power. From the beginning of the First Dynasty (c.3000–2890 BC) or even before, the living king was identified as the god Horus, son of Osiris, the deity who first ruled Egypt. He then attained 'great god' status upon death, when he became Osiris. Simultaneously, from an early era, kings began to assert that they were sons of the sun god Ra, and several went so far as to assert that Ra assumed human form to beget the future ruler with the queen. Did that mean that kings believed themselves to be gods? Rulers certainly knew they were mortal, and

examination of their mummified remains has painted a bleak picture of heart disease, arthritis and tooth abscesses. A few pharaohs declared themselves to be full gods even in life, such as Rameses II, who was even depicted worshipping himself. Evidence points, though, to a belief that their human nature was blended with a divine one. Kings used the title *neter nefer* to show their divine status; while *neter* signifies a deity, *nefer* ('good') adds a human element, lessening the divine status somewhat. They were major gods only after they died, and their successors and subjects frequently invoked them in prayer. The Middle Kingdom *Tale of Sinuhe*, which opens with a king's death, describes it as mounting to heaven and union with the sun.

It was their living status as a junior god that made it possible for pharaohs to serve as essential mediators between humans and gods, making the king both a god and a servant of the gods. Enemies of pharaoh were thus enemies of the gods. As the *Loyalist Teaching* proclaims, it is the duty of all to serve and praise the king, who sees all and illuminates Egypt more than the sun, providing sustenance and plenty.

CORONATION CEREMONIES

The great gods, the true rulers of Egypt, accepted the king as their legitimate representative with the coronation ritual. Our best sources for this event are inscriptions of Hatshepsut and Horemheb; since Hatshepsut was a woman and Horemheb a military commander of non-royal blood, both had a particular need to stress their legitimacy. The ceremony included a symbolic recreation of the union of Upper and Lower Egypt, a circuit of the walls, and solemn purification, upon which the gods of Egypt (with priests as their proxies) saluted the new king and welcomed him into the sacred circle. The new ruler was invested with the crowns of Egypt and regalia by priests who were probably enacting the parts of the deities Nekhen and Pe, the guardians of Upper and Lower Egypt. The Roman mystic Publius Nigidius Figulus, who saw

Kings' titles were bestowed during the coronation. For ancient Egyptians, the royal name was more like a sentence that revealed much about the monarch's political goals and worldview.

ABOVE: Amenhotep III, wearing the Blue Crown, which was especially associated with rulers of the New Kingdom in times of war.

OPPOSITE: Cartouche of Sety I. The king (and very rarely a queen consort) was marked as unique in inscriptions by having his name enclosed in an oblong knotted rope that represents infinity. The presence of cartouches, named after the distinctive ammunition cases of French troops, was the key to deciphering hieroglyphs.

a coronation in the 1st century BC, adds that the new king entered an inner sanctum, where he swore an oath to protect Egypt's land and water.

The regalia were laden with heavy ritual significance. The crowns, which were themselves regarded as deities, emphasized the unifying role of kingship. A king could don either the high white helmet-crown of Upper Egypt (the *hedjet*), the basket-shaped crown of Lower Egypt (the *deshret*) or the double crown that combined the two (the *pschent*). The Blue Crown (the *khepresh*) came to mark the pharaoh as the war leader in the New Kingdom, while for less formal occasions the ruler's head was covered with the *nemes*, a striped linen headcloth that only a king could wear. Crowns and *nemes* alike were adorned with the *uraeus*, the goddesses Wadjet and Nekhbet (patrons of Lower and Upper Egypt) in the forms of a cobra and a vulture, the cobra with hood raised, threatening Egypt's enemies. For formal audiences, the pharaoh bore a crook and flail, representing the ruler's duty to care for and protect his people. Egyptian men were clean-shaven, but believed that the gods wore beards, so the regalia also included a false beard made of gold and semi-precious stones.

The complex titles of a king were also bestowed during the coronation. Modern scholars usually just call pharaohs by their birth name, such as Amenhotep, Rameses or Sety. For ancient Egyptians, however, the royal name was more like a sentence that revealed much about the monarch's political goals and worldview. The so-called 'five-fold titulary', which was fully developed by the Fifth Dynasty (2494–2345 BC), also served as an ideological statement, as three of the titles stressed the ruler's role as a god, while two emphasized the union of Upper and Lower Egypt. First came the birth name, always accompanied by the title 'son of Ra'. The earliest additional title was the Horus name, which first appeared in the so-called Dynasty 0 (*c.*3200–3000 BC). The *nebty* name, 'he of the two ladies', placed the ruler under the protection of the goddesses Wadjet and Nekhbet of Upper and Lower Egypt. Fourth was the Horus of Gold name, which perhaps refers to Horus in his incarnation as a sun god. Finally came the *nesu-bit* throne name, always preceded by the phrase 'he who belongs to the sedge and the bee', the symbols of Upper and Lower Egypt. The last title also alludes to the

LEFT: **Queen Hatshepsut, depicted here as a male pharaoh, engaging in the run that was part of the** *sed* **festival's rituals. A scene from Hatshepsut's reconstructed Red Chapel, Karnak.**

ABOVE: **Egyptian priests maintained a facade of continuity by depicting Roman emperors as traditional pharaohs. Here Emperor Trajan makes an offering to the goddess Hathor, who is nursing her son Ihy. From the temple of Hathor at Dendera.**

king's unique blending of divine and mortal, since *nesu* refers to the unchanging divine king, while *bit* describes the current, ephemeral ruler. The new monarch would send a proclamation of his royal titles to officials through Egypt, who would then renew their oaths of office.

THE CONCEPT OF *MAAT*

A king's duty can be summed up as the need to uphold *maat*, which can be translated as cosmic order, truth and justice. As the Egyptians understood the world, *maat* was under constant threat from the forces of chaos (*isfet*). Yet if Egypt and its people were to prosper, *maat* must be preserved. Order meant unity, and only a king could keep Egypt unified. The preservation of *maat* also carried a sometimes-heavy burden of protection, so an important royal function was to defeat Egypt's enemies, whether on the battlefield or symbolically. Few kings missed the opportunity to portray themselves smiting Egypt's enemies with a mace, whether they had ever led a military expedition or not. Enforcing laws, controlling the greed of court officials, overseeing irrigation networks and maintaining the food supply were all royal duties subsumed under the principle of *maat*.

At least as important as administrative and military tasks, however, were the ritual acts that would preserve *maat* by keeping the gods content. The pharaoh, himself (or herself) a god, was a unique mediator between Egypt's gods and people. Pharaoh was the chief priest of every deity; although most daily sacrifices were delegated, with very rare exceptions only the king's name or image appeared in temples, which were themselves erected and maintained at the king's expense. The pharaohs were expected to be generous in their offerings to the gods; in return, the gods would provide for Egypt.

FESTIVALS AND RITUALS

Great festivals served both to present the ruler to the Egyptian people and to renew his link to the great gods. Most Egyptians would only have seen their king seated in glory on a boat, or carried from palace to temple on the backs of strong men. While there were many festive occasions, two in particular stand out, the *sed* and the *opet*. The *opet* festival was developed by the New Kingdom as an annual renewal of the king's divinity; in it, the king would process from Thebes to Luxor to commune with the gods, above all Amun. The *sed* festival by contrast was of great antiquity, first attested in the reign of Den in the First Dynasty, and celebrated throughout Egyptian history. A symbolic restoration of the ruler's physical and magical power, the ceremony was properly enacted in the 30th year of the king's reign (although some pharaohs cheated and held the festival earlier) and every three to ten years after that. The *sed* brought together images of the gods and their priests from all Egypt. Special buildings were created for the event, such as the *sed*-festival court built for Osorkon II at Bubastis, or the lake by Amenhotep III's palace at Malkata; the hieroglyph for the *sed* is an open-sided pavilion with two thrones. The five-day jubilee developed over the centuries, but the essential components were a ritual claim of territory as pharaoh proved his ongoing strength by running between markers that represented the borders of Egypt and then received his people's homage. In the course of the ceremony, the pharaoh would visit the shrines of various gods, hand out honours and gifts, and preside over a mock battle between followers of the gods Horus and Set.

The king's role as mediator and junior god meant that the ruler's life was hemmed around with never-ending ritual. The appearance of the ruler at temple ceremonies and state occasions was described as 'shining forth' (*khay*), the same word used for the sun at the dawn of creation. The late author Diodorus Siculus reports that all the details of a king's daily life were prescribed, making him a living fetish and constantly presenting the ruler as the living image of a god to those who saw him.

Palaces were very similar in layout to temples, divided into increasingly restricted areas with access to the king himself limited to those with the title 'friend of the king'. As with temples, those who came to the palace had to be ritually pure; as the victory stela of the Late Period (664–332 BC) King Piye proclaims, most of the king's former enemies, although pardoned, were barred from the palace because they were uncircumcised fish-eaters, suggesting some of these restrictions. Subjects, even the greatest nobles, who were admitted to the king's presence were expected to prostrate themselves and kiss the ground before their ruler. It was a great privilege to be allowed to kiss the king's foot; a Fifth Dynasty inscription in the tomb of the vizier Washptah tells that the

ABOVE: **Nefertari, the first great wife of Rameses II, here depicted playing senet. Nefertari's tomb is one of the most elaborately decorated in the Valley of the Queens at Thebes.**

whole court trembled with fear when they heard he had been granted the honour, and the favour was so extraordinary that the king ordered it inscribed in Washptah's tomb. The fictional character Sinuhe, when he returns from his long exile and is granted an audience with the king, simply faints.

OFFICIAL DUTIES

Administration of the state was inseparable from tending to a pharaoh's personal needs. The central government included offices for foreign affairs, the military, the treasury, public works, granaries, armouries, mortuary cults of kings and the regulation of temple priesthoods, all under the supervision of the vizier. Yet even the most important officials also held offices that sound menial to the modern ear, although the actual duties may have been delegated. For example, Pepy I's vizier was 'controller of the king's kilt', while under Merneri a royal sandal-bearer went on to be governor of all Upper Egypt. On the walls of noble tombs, the incumbents proudly proclaim their offices, including a royal manicurist and a 'chief of the butchers', besides more obvious titles, such as that of Hesy-Ra of the Third Dynasty (2686–2613 BC), 'overseer of the royal scribes, greatest of physicians and dentists'.

The personal staff of the king and his family was elaborate and would have numbered hundreds of cooks, barbers, cup-bearers, entertainers and all the services needed to maintain large and elaborate palaces. Members of the royal family could become very close to these officials/servitors. One Old Kingdom ruler, for instance, cared greatly for his vizier Westptah. When the old man collapsed while attending the king, physicians were summoned but could not save him. The king was inconsolable, ordering the ritual purification of the body to be carried out in his own presence and giving specific orders for Westptah's burial, including provision of an ebony coffin.

Many of those servitors would have been employed in the women's quarters, the *per-khenret*, often simply known by the modern term 'harem'. The harem had its own organized bureaucracy from an early time, employing scribes, craftsmen and entertainers. Unlike most Egyptian men, pharaohs were polygamous; after all, it was essential to secure the succession, besides the fact that multiple sexual partners have always been a symbol of male power. One of the king's women would be designated as the 'great wife' – if she had a son, he would be the natural heir. In addition, there were lesser wives. Sometimes married to cement foreign alliances or to honour an Egyptian noble family, the number of women in the harem tended to swell over time; Rameses II in the New Kingdom (1550–1069 BC) probably had up to 200 wives and concubines at a time.

Polygamy of course carried its risk, and we know of several harem plots as the king's women vied to win the throne for their own sons. Accounts of these plots demonstrate that the women's quarters were far from isolated; Rameses III's minor wife Tiye plotted with 28 high court and military officials. It should be emphasized that *sometimes* the king married a half or full sister, a practice that can be seen most clearly in the Fourth Dynasty (2613–2494 BC) and Twelfth Dynasty (1985–1773 BC). Not a custom for non-royal Egyptians, such marriages probably served at least in part to display the king's divinity, replicating the marriage of divine brothers and sisters at the time of creation. These brother–sister matings were most common after periods of disunity, helping to re-establish the king's divinity as quickly as possible.

BELOW: **Calcite wedding casket found in the tomb of Tutankhamun. It is engraved with the cartouches of both Tutankhamun and his sister-wife Ankhesenamun. Wrapped in linen within the small chest were two balls of hair, apparently that of the couple. Howard Carter believed it marked the marriage contract between the two.**

DAWN OF THE GOD-KINGS

The origins of kingship in Egypt are hidden in the mists of time. By about 5000 BC, archaeologists have found evidence of regional rulers – for example, when elaborate tombs with imported wood walls suggest people of special importance. Then at least in Upper Egypt (the upper Nile region, in the south of the country), the regions began to coalesce into a single state. We do not know if this unification of Upper Egypt was violent or peaceful. The rulers of Nekhen became especially important. Nekhen was the chief centre for the worship of the hawk-god Horus, and its identification with Horus remained so strong that the Greeks dubbed the city Hierakonpolis, 'the city of the hawk'. Besides an important early temple of Horus, archaeologists have discovered there a ceremonial hub, with an oval courtyard measuring 41.1 x 12.2m (135 x 40ft), that was used for about 500 years before Egypt's earliest recognized dynasty emerged.

OPPOSITE: **The pyramids of Menkaura, Khafra and Khufu at Giza, with subsidiary pyramids for royal wives. These monuments from the Fourth Dynasty are the greatest of Egypt's 70 surviving pyramids, and were all constructed in the 26th century BC.**

RIGHT: **Ceremonial macehead, depicting the early ruler known only as 'the Scorpion King' (from the scorpion symbol beside his carved face). The king, ceremonially crowned and wearing a bull's tail, is probably ritually opening an irrigation channel with a hoe.**

EARLY RULERS

A series of important discoveries since the 1960s have led scholars to designate a significant 'Dynasty 0' (c.3200–3000 BC) in the south before the unification of Upper and Lower Egypt. The invention of hieroglyphic writing by about 3250 BC allows us to attach names to the last four of these early rulers – Scorpion, Iri-Hor, Ka and Narmer. The ruler known as Scorpion was clearly an important man. His tomb at Abydos was a palace for the dead, with 12 chambers laid out like the rooms of a royal residence. Although looted in antiquity, archaeologists still found at the site more than 400 Palestinian wine jars, evidence that the ruler had the resources to bring goods from a long distance. They also discovered an ivory *heka* sceptre, the crook that later served as a major symbol of kingship and may already have been used that way in the 4th millennium. From about the same period, we have an important artefact associated with what was probably a different ruler also identified with the hieroglyph for 'scorpion' – a ceremonial macehead, found in the temple area of Hierakonpolis. A king is depicted on the macehead in full ritual clothing, including a bull's tail hanging from the back of his belt and the white crown of Upper Egypt, strongly implying that he ruled the entirety of the south. Further evidence of this consolidation is that King Ka was the first to have his name placed in a *serekh*, the outline of a building with a niched facade and a falcon mounted on the top, which continued as a symbol of royalty until it was replaced by the cartouche.

Upper and Lower Egypt became a single kingdom, and the pharaohs of the united land emphasized the significance of that union.

Unlike the south, Lower Egypt apparently did not come together as a single kingdom before Upper Egypt's conquest. No named rulers are known from the north, although admittedly in the wetter conditions of the Nile Delta, tombs and other sites are not nearly as well preserved as in the drier south. The concept of Lower Egypt as a distinct kingdom was probably an invention for political and religious purposes. After all, Upper and Lower did in time become a single kingdom, and the pharaohs of the united land constantly emphasized the significance of that union in their titles and other symbols of rule. King Djet in the First Dynasty (c.3000–2890 BC) was apparently the first ruler to combine the crowns of the two regions into a single double crown.

The late historian Manetho names a King Menes as the great unifier and places him at the head of the First Dynasty. Egyptologists identify this figure with either Narmer or Narmer's successor Aha. Uniting all Egypt was actually

gradual, however, with several southern kings adding northern territory by conquest or diplomacy. It has been suggested that Scorpion I began the unification with wars that gained him territory as far as modern Cairo. There is in fact little evidence for military conquest beyond what may be purely symbolic military scenes on a number of ceremonial objects. The Narmer macehead, for example, shows the king capturing an implausibly large force of 120,000 men as well as 1,422,000 goats, while the Narmer Palette depicts him wearing the crown of Upper Egypt on one side and of Lower Egypt on the other. The process was certainly drawn-out, and although kings could claim to rule all Egypt by *c*.3000 BC, several First Dynasty rulers had to reinforce the lesson of unity; Anedjib, fifth king of that dynasty (*c*.2700 BC) was probably the first to be recognized as king by all regions. As the Intermediate Periods demonstrate, the union of Upper and Lower Egypt was by no means natural and inevitable. Although they shared the Nile and a common language, north and south were geographically distinct. The arid south had access to the gold and other products of East Africa, while the wetter north looked towards West Asia and the Mediterranean.

BELOW: **The Narmer Palette is one of the most significant finds from early Egypt. Crafted from siltstone, it was one of the earliest depictions of an Egyptian king. The Palette depicts a triumph, whether actual or symbolic, and presents the king wearing on one side the crown of Upper Egypt and on the reverse that of Lower Egypt.**

TOTEMIC TOMBS OF THE FIRST DYNASTY

The kings of the First Dynasty, starting in *c*.3000 BC, took a series of steps to consolidate their rule of the united Egypt. Aha, Narmer's probable son and successor, was the most significant of these rulers. Aha, which means 'the fighter', is actually this monarch's Horus name, taken on accession; we don't know his birth name. Such a name choice was programmatic; his reign probably included fighting within Egypt as well as an expedition into Nubia. King Aha apparently came to the throne as a child, with his mother Neithhotep serving as regent, suggesting both a degree of stability and respect for the sacred royal bloodline. Aha certainly emphasized the unique importance of the monarchy; his tomb at Abydos was five times as large as his father's. Aha's most important achievement was the construction of a new capital, Memphis, demonstrating the shift of

Although they shared the Nile and a common language, north and south were geographically distinct.

royal attention towards the north. The site, just south of the Nile Delta not far south of modern Cairo, was clearly chosen for its political importance; legend tells that Aha even had to divert the course of the Nile and reclaim the land on which to build the city. Originally called Ineb-hedj (the 'white-walled', after its plastered mudbrick walls), over time people started referring to this capital as Men-nefer-Mare after Pepy I's pyramid complex nearby; the Greeks altered that to Memphis.

Egyptian palaces, built of mudbrick, have left hardly a trace behind, but fortunately rulers (and their officials) were more concerned for durability in their tombs, which were intended to serve as homes for eternity. The kings of the early period and Old Kingdom put enormous resources into the creation of sumptuous and increasingly impressive tombs, giving a skewed impression of the life-loving Egyptians but also providing a great deal of evidence for modern scholars. The First Dynasty chose Abydos for burials, a site sacred to the god of the dead even before the cult of Osiris developed. Indeed, the tomb of one First Dynasty king, Djer, was later identified with the tomb of

BELOW: **Detail of one of the four bracelets found in the tomb of King Djer at Abydos. It consists of a row of *serekhs*, a palace facade surmounted by the Horus hawk; the *serekh* enclosed the king's name in early Egypt.**

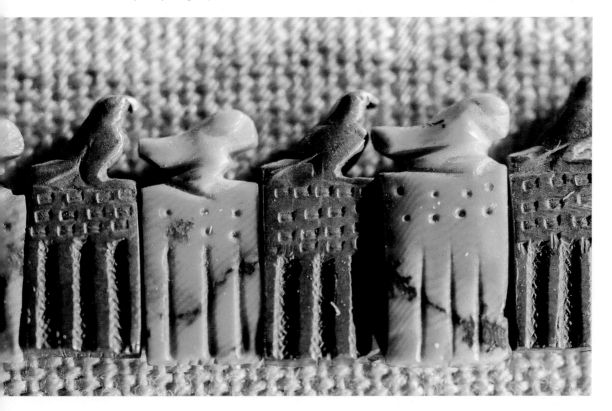

Osiris himself. Except for a mummified arm found in the tomb of Djer, the rulers' remains were no longer in the tombs when uncovered by modern archaeologists. All had been plundered in antiquity, and there is evidence of burning, suggesting that the mummified remains were purposely destroyed to deny the kings an afterlife.

The royal cemetery at Abydos clearly shows the ideology of kingship. The tombs' monumental architecture strongly supports the notion of a state religion dedicated to worshipping deceased god-kings; beside the tombs themselves were substantial mortuary cult buildings to assure perpetual offerings and worship. Although the tombs were looted, what remains demonstrates the kings' control of massive resources, including foreign luxury goods and raw materials; they probably also commanded conscript labour to do the building and excavating involved. Strikingly, the burial chambers, made of mudbrick in deep pits, were lined with cedar, which had to be imported from western Asia. Aha had access to logs long enough to have 5.5m (18ft)-long architectural beams installed in his tomb, suggesting that he controlled sizeable ships on the Mediterranean. And indeed, we can see the remnants of these early pharaohs' boats. Over a dozen ships were buried near Abydos, each between 15.2 and 18.3m (50–60ft) long, each enclosed in a brick 'coffin' within a burial pit. Such ships were probably intended to convey the dead ruler to the afterlife.

The most flagrant consumption of all was human: the kings of the First Dynasty were buried with numerous attendants, almost certainly killed to go with their ruler and serve him in death as they had in life. King Aha was accompanied in death by 36 other human bodies, ranged in three rows around the royal burial chamber. All were men aged between 20 and 30 years. Although the state of their remains makes it impossible to know how they died, the suggestion that they were the royal bodyguard is compelling. Aha's subsidiary burials also included at least seven large cats, probably his hunting leopards. By the time of Djer, the numbers had risen significantly. No fewer than 318 small chambers were found around Djer's burial chamber for subsidiary burials. Although the site has been much disturbed, about 100 of these chambers still held limestone

BELOW: Boats were important funeral gear, and a number of river vessels have been found at Abydos. Here can be seen 5,000-year-old remains of several boats that had been buried in their own mudbrick tombs, near those of a pharaoh.

ROYAL WOMEN

For the most part, the queens and princesses of ancient Egypt are little more than names. A few women, however, achieved public prominence thanks to biological accident, when no adult male was available to rule. The earliest woman of Egypt we can see at all clearly is Merneith of the First Dynasty. She was the wife of King Djet and, when her husband died, she served as regent for their young son, Den. Merneith was clearly a person of power; indeed, it was only recently proven that she was a woman, when a jar seal was discovered that named her as the king's mother.

Merneith had some of the prerogatives of a king rather than a consort, reflecting her years of independent rule. Her tomb at Abydos, beside that of her husband, was sumptuous and well-built. Also, unlike the tombs of other royal females of the age, Merneith enjoyed the honour of companions in the afterlife. Forty-one subsidiary burials were found around her tomb. It seems clear that they were her servants in this life and were intended to continue serving in the next. A number were artisans, with the tools of their trades beside them, such as paints with the artist and vases with the potter.

RIGHT: One of two steles found at the tomb of Queen Merneith at Abydos. Merneith was buried in a large funerary complex beside the tombs of kings, adding to speculation that she ruled Egypt independently for a number of years.

steles with names, and sometimes also titles, suggesting elite status. About 85 per cent of the names found there were women. The clearest evidence that these people buried around the king were human sacrifices comes from the tomb of Semerkhet. The royal burial chamber and its 69 subsidiary graves were all covered by the same roof, so the bodies must have been interred at the same time. The practice of sending servants to the afterlife with the ruler ended with the First Dynasty; the last king of that dynasty, Qa'a, had only 26 tomb-companions.

CONSOLIDATION AND REUNIFICATION IN THE SECOND DYNASTY (2890–2686 BC)

The fact that all the tombs of First Dynasty pharaohs were gutted by fire, perhaps as early as the Second Dynasty, helps demonstrate that the path of unification and order did not run smoothly. The Second Dynasty's history is very obscure, but there are other hints of disorder and perhaps outright civil war. The tombs of the first three rulers of the dynasty were located at Saqqara, further to the north, rather than Abydos, suggesting that perhaps the kings were from that region. At least some of them certainly did not identify with Hierakonpolis and its worship of the god Horus, who had already been identified in the First Dynasty as the prime god of kingship. One Second

BELOW: **Horus, the most important god of kingship, from a wall painting in the Valley of the Kings. He holds an ankh, the sign of life, and wears the *pschent*, the double crown that symbolized both Upper and Lower Egypt.**

Dynasty pharaoh, Peribsen, went so far as to top the *serekh* that enclosed his name with the mythical animal representing the god Set instead of the Horus hawk. While Set did not become identified as evil until the New Kingdom (1550–1069 BC), already in this early period the story had developed of how Set tricked and killed Osiris, and was then locked in a long struggle with Osiris' heir Horus, until finally the council of gods assigned Horus the rule of Egypt and gave Set control of the desert regions. Horus eventually passed the rule of Egypt to human kings, who at least in part became avatars of Horus. That Peribsen identified himself with Set was thus a clear rejection of much of the ideology of kingship.

The next and last ruler of the Second Dynasty was responsible for reunification. He is known only by his Horus name, Khasekhem ('the power has appeared'), but partway through his reign took the unusual step of changing that name to Khasekhemwy, ('the *two* powers have appeared'). When Khasekhemwy first came to the throne, there appears to have been a different king ruling in Lower Egypt, and from his base in the south Khasekhemwy launched a violent war to regain control

Mining and foreign trade were in royal hands and were manipulated to concentrate wealth at the top of society.

ABOVE: **Much of the mudbrick wall surrounding Khasekhemwy's enormous mortuary complex at Abydos still survives and has been restored thanks to a major conservation project that began in 1999 and still continues today.**

of the whole land. The base of a statue commemorating his victory over Lower Egypt has an inscription proclaiming that 47,209 northern 'rebels' were killed in the campaign. Certainly, by the time of Khasekhemwy's death in c.2650 BC, Egypt was finally truly united. His tomb at Abydos still hints at this king's power. Khasekhemwy's remains were interred in a limestone-lined burial chamber, surrounded by no fewer than 58 storage rooms, providing enough space to hold all the grave goods of the First Dynasty combined. Although robbers had looted the tomb, modern excavators found large amounts of tools and pottery, as well as small decorative items such as beads. Archaeologists also discovered a sceptre crafted from gold and sard.

TRADE AND MILITARY EXPEDITIONS IN THE EARLY DYNASTIC PERIOD (C.3000–2686 BC)

Several points are clear about the Early Dynastic Period. Most obvious, thanks to the evidence of the tombs, is that rulers were able to control resources to an astonishing degree. Already in the First Dynasty, the court tracked the height of the Nile's annual inundation, since the level of the flood indicated how good the harvest would be and tax rates could be set accordingly. Mining and foreign trade were also in royal hands and manipulated to concentrate wealth at the top of society. From the time of unification, the royal administration kept control of trade routes reaching both southwards into Nubia and northwards to the Near East; traded products, whether Nubian gold, Lebanese cedar or fine Palestinian wine, were hoarded in great quantities in the royal tombs and would certainly have adorned the pharaohs' lives as well. Besides trade, the kings also employed prospectors to find the mineral wealth of the less-populated lands beyond the Nile, especially to the east. Large expeditions were sent to open and work mines on a temporary basis and, again, the fruits of their labours would come to the pharaoh.

This determination to exploit resources also led to conflict. We cannot know if or when the kings themselves bore weapons in battle, but they certainly committed troops to war, and their position as 'commander in chief' can be seen from the royal sceptre in the form of a mace (the *ames*), which was employed as a symbol of rule starting in *c.*3000 BC. While wretched captives were a popular art theme throughout ancient Egyptian history, certainly at least sometimes they represented real enemies rather than simply serving as a metaphor for the forces of chaos. In the Early Dynastic Period, the challenge was above all to protect the routes of trade expeditions. For example, in the reign of King Den, the Palermo Stone reports considerable military activity, such as 'the year of the smiting of the Asiatics', which is most likely a reference to desert-dwellers to the northeast. Djer, by contrast, launched military campaigns westwards against the Libyans.

BELOW: The Palermo Stone is the largest fragment of a stela that probably dates to the Fifth Dynasty. It lists the kings of Egypt from the First Dynasty up to its own time, along with brief notes about their reigns, such as the height of the Nile's flood and major festivals. Interestingly, it also includes the mothers of pharaohs, suggesting that mothers played a significant role in the royal court.

Nubia was, as throughout later history, a particularly high priority because of its gold. The kings of the early period established direct rule as far south as the first cataract of the Nile, as can be seen from seal impressions with Peribsen's name found at Elephantine. At least some rulers pushed further south than that, however, establishing an outpost at Buhen between the first and second cataracts as early as the Second Dynasty. Khasekhemwy at the end of the Early Dynastic Period took advantage of internal peace to launch a major military expedition into Nubia. More than just a raid, the king had important mines fortified and garrisons established at trading posts. But the goal remained exploitation of resources rather than rule; Khasekhemwy's force did not push into Nubia's hinterland.

PYRAMIDS AND POWER IN THE THIRD DYNASTY (2686–2613 BC)

With Khasekhemwy's death we move to the period 19th-century scholars designated as the Old Kingdom, most commonly reckoned as lasting from 2686 to 2160 BC and including the Third through Eighth Dynasties. There was no clear break between the Second and Third Dynasties; the first official ruler of the Old Kingdom was Khasekhemwy's heir. But there is no denying that the importance of rulers moved from impressive to awe-inspiring. The Old Kingdom was the great age of pyramid construction, imitated but not equalled in the Twelfth Dynasty (1985–1773 BC). As monuments to how completely a ruler could control the resources of his land, only the tomb of the first emperor of China can compare.

Djoser, the first pharaoh of the Third Dynasty, certainly thought big. His architect and vizier, Imhotep (who was later deified as a god of architecture and healing), created the first entirely stone building in the world, the Step Pyramid at Saqqara. It began as a tomb of the type known as a *mastaba*, essentially a large rectangular box. But then a second stone box was placed atop the first, until a total of six layers formed a monumental staircase to

ABOVE: The Step Pyramid of Djoser. The Third Dynasty moved its necropolis to Saqqara, and this great stone structure dominates the site. It is part of an enormous mortuary complex that attests to the resources of the Old Kingdom. Much of the rock was quarried on site, as a great trench dug into the bedrock around the mortuary complex attests.

heaven. The entire edifice originally stood 62.2m (204ft) tall and was faced with limestone. The pyramid itself has an elaborate substructure of shafts sunk 27.4m (90ft) deep and tunnels that run over 4.8km (3 miles); the subterranean burial vault was lined with granite and green faience tiles. As with all of Egypt's pyramids, the Step Pyramid was surrounded by a large complex of buildings; the whole limestone-paved enclosure covered 149,734 sq m (37 acres). This great mortuary complex called for at least as much labour as the tomb itself. It was enclosed by a high wall of dressed stone, studded with 211 bastions, and the wall was then surrounded by a great ditch, 24.4m (80ft) deep and 39.6m (130ft) wide. Buildings included 25 chapels laid out for the *sed* festival as well as a *sed* court.

It is obvious that Djoser controlled immense resources, but what can we know of him and his successors as human beings? Far from being hated for his exactions, Egyptians of later era remembered Djoser as the paragon of a wise and pious king. Even that, however, may be a later invention; Djoser's name means 'sacred', and subsequent writers may have simply invented a character to fit the name. Djoser's posthumous reputation is, however, a useful reminder that we should not assume that pharaohs were tyrants who not only siphoned a lion's share of wealth from their land but forced their subjects to

The pyramid became a symbol of royal authority that went well beyond the actual burial of the ruler...

labour on massive monuments like the Step Pyramid. Much of the wealth the rulers garnered would have been redistributed to the populace – for example, as rations for the people who laboured on large building projects during the months when the Nile's inundation made work on their own farms impossible. Similarly, we know that Sekhemkhet, Djoser's successor, sent one of the first expeditions to exploit the turquoise mines of the Sinai Peninsula. While it is unlikely that many of the miners and guards sent on this venture got any of the semi-precious stone for themselves, they would have received rations and other rewards.

The fate of Sekhemkhet's tomb illustrates a recurring difficulty of the age of pyramids. An unfinished step pyramid intended for his burial was discovered at Saqqara in 1951. Sekhemkhet had clearly decided to do one better than his predecessor, and a massive platform – 518 x 182m (1,700 x 600ft) – was constructed above a substructure. The pyramid was never completed, however, probably because Sekhemkhet ruled for only six years. His successor would have devoted all the labour resources at his command to construction

of his own tomb; the amount of labour a pharaoh could command was finite. Even Sekhemkhet's burial chamber was left unfinished, although a massive one-piece alabaster sarcophagus was found there, with no sign of robbers. One of the many mysteries of early Egypt is what happened to Sekhemkhet himself; when the sarcophagus was opened in 1954, it was empty.

The pyramid became a symbol of royal authority that went well beyond the actual burial of the ruler (and, in time, favoured wives). Pyramids were proclamations of royal power, as can be seen by the Third Dynasty's construction of a series of smaller step pyramids, standing 9.1–15.2m (30–50ft) high, that were not used for burial. Seven of these edifices have been found, as far south as Elephantine and up to the Faiyum in Middle Egypt. They stood outside important early towns, probably capitals of the administrative districts (*nomes*) of the period. At the same time, kings and their architects pushed towards ever more impressive royal tombs. The last pharaoh of the Third Dynasty was responsible for the Meidum Pyramid, the first pyramid with a square ground plan. Constructed originally with seven tall steps (three still remain), loose stones were then packed in the steps, and the whole structure covered with white limestone. Although the outer skins have collapsed, the Meidum Pyramid still stands 65.2m (214ft) tall and must have been massively more impressive than Djoser's tomb.

BELOW: The Meidum Pyramid in Lower Egypt was perhaps built for Huni, last king of the Third Dynasty. It was originally intended as a true pyramid, with limestone fill over the rock core. Perhaps never completed, now all that remains is the stone core; its appearance is so odd that in Arabic it is called the 'False Pyramid'.

SNEFERU – A MODEL OF KINGSHIP

With the Fourth Dynasty (2613–2494 BC) pharaohs – Sneferu, Khufu, Djedefra, Khafra, Menkaura and Shepseskaf – we enter more visibly than ever an age of god-kings. Sneferu was the first to have his name on inscriptions enclosed within a cartouche, the symbol of eternity. Djedefra went still further by adopting 'son of Ra' as a royal title. These rulers constructed the greatest of Egypt's more than 70 pyramids, so it is hardly surprising that stories came to be attached to their names. We also have more evidence from sources contemporary to them, ranging from inscriptions at mines to labels in noble tombs. As a result, they emerge at least somewhat from the shadows of antiquity, although it is often impossible to separate fact from later Egyptian fiction.

Sneferu took the Horus name 'Lord of *Maat*', suggesting that he was restoring order and that the Third Dynasty had ended in civil disruption. Although the new king was a member of the extended royal family, he was not

ABOVE: **Quartzite head of Djedefra, found at Abu Rawash. Little remains today of the pyramid constructed for this king of the Fourth Dynasty because the Romans reused most of its stone.**

OVERLEAF: **The Red Pyramid at Dahshur is the third largest of Egypt's pyramids. It was the final pyramid erected by Sneferu and was probably the first 'true' pyramid, planned from the start with smooth sides. It was originally white, but the limestone casing was used in constructing Cairo, exposing the red stone below.**

BUILDING THE PYRAMIDS

It was the labour of free subjects that constructed the pyramids, not foreign slaves. Among the resources the pharaohs controlled was the right to demand labour of their non-noble subjects, female as well as male. Only priests and scribes were exempted from this duty to the state. Men could be conscripted to serve in the army or on mining and trade expeditions, but above all they were needed as builders, with women providing support services in the labour camps. We can still see traces of what must have been a highly elaborate administrative structure, centrally controlled but organized through the towns.

Once the workers had arrived on site, they required housing and massive storehouses must have been built to provide their rations of bread, onions and beer. Since most of these structures were built of mudbrick, little trace has survived. That said, excavators have uncovered one workers' village south of Menkaura's pyramid, which included dormitories for about 4,000 people; there must have been others, since it is estimated that if construction went on year-round, it would have required about 25,000 people at a time working in three-month shifts to bring the pyramid to completion. The Great Pyramid of Khufu probably needed even more manpower and 20 years of continuous labour.

Were pharaoh's subjects happy to serve, rejoicing perhaps in the spiritual rewards they would receive when the king died and became a full god? Surely some did regard their labour as appropriate service of the god-king. Many must have also been happy to receive an assured food supply in the months of the Nile inundation; the employment of massive numbers of workers was probably beneficial for the Egyptian economy as a whole. The harsh punishments of those who evaded labour service clearly show that not everyone was overjoyed at the prospect of hauling stones for pharaoh, however. Not just the absconder himself but his family and anyone who helped his evasion were punished. We have records from the fortress of Askut in Lower Nubia telling that evaders were sent there for very undesirable garrison duty; probably others were consigned to the quarries.

Khufu's Great Pyramid originally stood at 146.6m (481ft), making it the tallest structure in the world until the completion of the 169m (555ft)-tall Washington Monument in 1884.

OPPOSITE: 'The Building of the Pyramids' by Gustav Richter is this 19th-century German artist's largest work, painted for the Maximilianeum in Munich. It displays well the fascination of the time with the monuments of ancient Egypt.

Later ages remembered Sneferu with fondness. The rulers of the Twelfth Dynasty looked to him as a model of kingship.

his predecessor Huni's son, although he married Huni's daughter Hetepheres, probably to consolidate his claim. As pharaoh, Sneferu established his dynasty's practice of keeping Egypt's important administrative posts in the family. For example, Sneferu's son Ankhkhaf served as royal vizier. Sneferu also appears to have been eager to develop foreign trade beyond what his predecessors had done. The Palermo Stone reports the construction of ships and import of 40 boatloads of cedar (probably from Byblos) in the 13th year of his reign. Sneferu also ordered military expeditions against both Libya and Nubia. Perhaps most striking in economic terms was the intensive working of the Sinai's turquoise mines, which was so successful that Sneferu was adopted as the patron god of the region.

Many of the resources of the state, whether from taxation on his subjects or trade, went into the building of no fewer than *three* pyramids. Sneferu completed his father-in-law's pyramid at Meidum, then went on to construct two more great pyramids at Dahshur. The work demonstrates both massive control of labour and building materials and rapid architectural innovation. The Meidum pyramid was the first true pyramidal structure, on a square base and with fill between the steps making its faces even. The Bent Pyramid at Dahshur took matters further, but apparently the angle that was originally planned put too great a strain on the foundation stones and had to be changed partway through construction, giving this pyramid its distinctive 'bent' shape. Perhaps because he was discontented with the effect, Sneferu then undertook yet another edifice, the Red Pyramid of Dahshur. It is estimated that these three pyramids between them required about 3.5 million cubic metres

(124 million cubic feet) of stone. The quarrying of stone, transport and setting the blocks in place would have been a massive undertaking even with modern automated equipment.

Nonetheless, later ages remembered Sneferu with fondness. The rulers of the Twelfth Dynasty looked to him as a model of kingship, deifying Sneferu and choosing to be buried near him at Dahshur. The Greeks who much later reported that Sneferu had been kind and benevolent must have heard about him from traditions preserved in the temples. We also have a tale from the Middle Kingdom (2055–1650 BC), preserved in the Westcar Papyrus, that presents Sneferu as a good-humoured, kindly man. The story opens with a striking image of the bored king wandering around the palace looking for entertainment. The vizier suggests a special outing: the king should be rowed on the lake by 20 beautiful young women of the palace, who moreover should be clad only in fishnets. So Sneferu started enjoying his outing, only to be jarred because one of the women lost her pendant in the water and stopped rowing. Instead of being angry, the king simply offered to replace it, but no, she wanted that particular adornment back. So, Sneferu summoned the court magician, who parted the water and retrieved the pendant.

ABOVE: Modern copy of a painting from the tomb of the Fourth Dynasty vizier Nefermaat and his wife Itet at Meidum. It is one of the earliest and finest examples of the waterfowl who were often depicted in tombs.

KHUFU'S ENDURING LEGACY

It is not clear why the memory of Sneferu's son Khufu is so much darker; perhaps the sheer scale of Khufu's Great Pyramid made later ages assume that it could only have been constructed at the expense of his people. Herodotus tells that both Khufu and Khafra (whose pyramid is the second largest) were tyrants who ruthlessly exploited the people of Egypt. It is hard to know what to make of such an assertion, which is not supported by either archaeological or textual evidence closer in time to the Old Kingdom. At least we can certainly discount the Greek story that Khufu's daughter was forced to prostitute herself to raise money to finish his pyramid, each client

paying with a stone. Khufu's Great Pyramid, the only wonder of the ancient world still standing, is certainly breathtaking in its grandeur. It originally stood at 146.6m (481ft), making it the tallest structure in the world until the completion of the 169m (555ft)-tall Washington Monument in 1884. The pyramid was built using an estimated 2.3 million stone blocks, averaging 2.3 tonnes (2.5 tons) but weighing up to 13.6 tonnes (15 tons). Originally, the whole pyramid would have been faced with limestone blocks, but almost all of the pyramid's skin found a second life in the construction of Cairo. The whole mortuary complex covered 53,014 sq m (13.1 acres). It was so thoroughly

endowed, or Khufu was held in such high esteem, that the mortuary rites continued there until the Twenty-sixth Dynasty (664–525 BC), nearly 2,000 years later. Despite elaborate defences, tomb robbers bored through the solid stone in antiquity and no trace of Khufu's body remains in his broken granite sarcophagus.

We can see a little of Khufu's family life. He appears to have held his mother Hetepheres in high esteem. He provided a small pyramid as her tomb. Although grave robbers soon broke in, they were apparently interrupted, and most of the grave goods were reinterred in a shaft tomb that remained

ABOVE: **The Great Pyramid of Giza, constructed for Khufu. As this photograph shows, modern Cairo has expanded to the very edge of the Giza necropolis, and much of the stone from the pharaohs' mortuary structures found its way into the buildings of medieval Cairo.**

untouched until George Reisner excavated it in the 1920s. A great gathering of dignitaries assembled for the opening of Hetepheres' apparently untouched sarcophagus, only to discover that it was empty. Khufu also had at least three major wives and constructed small pyramids for two of them. A son by a lesser wife, Menkhaf, served as vizier, continuing the dynasty's tradition of keeping important administrative positions in the family. Unfortunately, Khufu's polygamy led to infighting in the royal family. Prince Kewab was named heir but was killed, so the son of a rival wife inherited. The next two kings were half-brothers, and Egyptologists have suggested that Djedefra's decision to build his pyramid at Abu Roash rather than Giza is a sign of religious schism between the branches of Khufu's family. When Djedefra's half-brother Khafra took the throne, he displaced Djedefra's own three sons; a further sign of family disharmony is that the new pharaoh did not complete his brother's pyramid.

The Fourth Dynasty tended to keep important administrative positions in the family.

LATER FOURTH DYNASTY PHARAOHS

Little evidence of Khafra's reign survives beyond a vast burial complex that rivalled that of his father. The full complex included a temple in the valley, linked to a mortuary temple by a causeway, and a pyramid that, while not quite as tall as Khufu's, appears higher because it was constructed on rising ground. The work was extravagant, including great granite slabs as facing on the valley temple, which had to be transported from Aswan 965km (600 miles) upriver. The complex also includes the Sphinx, mostly carved from a natural rock outcropping, with paws of brick. The Sphinx' face is generally believed to be a portrait of Khafra.

The last of the three major pyramids at Giza was erected for Menkaure, the final ruler of the Fourth Dynasty. Although the smallest of the three, its interior has retained the most original decoration, with reliefs imitating the walls of an Old Kingdom palace. Herodotus, reporting much later, says that Menkaura was just and pious. Indeed, there is a legend that this king's benevolence offended the gods, who had ordained 150 years of hardship for Egypt and had their plans thwarted by the king's care for his people. The oracle at Buto, we are told, declared that Menkaura would only reign six years, but the highly dedicated king tried to double the accomplishments of his reign by staying awake nights as well as days. Manetho by contrast credits Menkaura with a reign of 63 years; in actuality he was probably on the throne for 28.

OPPOSITE: Gold pendant of Queen Hetepheres, who was probably the mother of Khufu. The queen's sarcophagus and burial furnishings were discovered in a pit tomb in 1925. Although her sarcophagus was empty, the furniture and other grave goods give valuable insight into the Old Kingdom court.

TRADE IN THE OLD KINGDOM

ABOVE: Fragment of a limestone relief depicting a trade expedition to Punt. Although this fragment from Hatshepsut's temple at Deir el-Bahri dates to the Eighteenth Dynasty, it was probably copied from an Old Kingdom relief.

Pharaohs did not just build pyramids and other elaborate tombs. They also devoted considerable resources to infrastructure that would make large-scale trade possible. Most notably, Old Kingdom rulers created two Red Sea ports. The older, at Wadi el-Jarf, is the oldest known artificial harbour in the world. Partially excavated in the 1950s, the site has been systematically explored since 2011. The creation of the port probably dates to the reign of Sneferu. The site was carefully chosen at a break in the barrier reef and provided with a natural well. A stone jetty measuring more than 183 x 183m (600 x 600ft) was built, and clearly saw significant Red Sea traffic; over 100 anchors have been found there. The whole town site extends well over 1.6km (1 mile), and a system of galleries for storage was carved into a nearby mountain, the chambers lined with limestone blocks to help

preserve valuable cargoes before they were carried overland to the Nile. The Wadi el-Jarf port operated for about 80 years before it was replaced by a newly constructed port further north at Ayn Soukhna. Both harbours were bases for trade as far south as Punt, which was probably located in modern Eritrea or Somalia. Trade was significant; the Palermo Stone tells of the arrival of 80,000 measures of what was probably myrrh in the reign of King Sahura of the Fifth Dynasty (2494–2345 BC).

Trade via the Red Sea remained dangerous, not just because of the conditions on that treacherous body of water but because the rulers of the Old Kingdom never completely controlled the eastern desert, home of nomadic 'sand-dwellers'. One text from late in the Old Kingdom reports that a force of these sand people massacred an entire expedition on the Red Sea coast as they prepared to sail to Punt.

The exotic riches of the south – above all the large quantities of incense essential for worship of the pharaoh and other gods – assured that the kings continued to invest in ports and expeditions. They also took great pride in these trade expeditions to the mysterious south. It is now thought that the famous reliefs at Deir el-Bahri depicting an expedition to Punt in the New Kingdom reign of Hatshepsut were actually copied from an Old Kingdom template. In other words, it was a venture worth boasting about in stone for over a thousand years.

GRIPPING ON TO POWER IN THE FIFTH DYNASTY

By the time the Fifth Dynasty came to power in *c.*2494 BC, the state was becoming too complex to be ruled as a family affair. More and more non-royals were installed in even the highest offices, perhaps in part a reaction to collateral branches of the royal family threatening the stability of the throne itself. It is possible that nervousness about overreach by male members of the family led the pharaohs to rely more on the royal women. At least the evidence from their tombs shows that two queens, both named Khentkawes, held real royal power. Khentkawes I, principal wife of Userkaf, appears in her tomb with the royal regalia and title. Similarly, Shepseskara's queen Khentkawes II, a granddaughter of Khufu, had honours reserved for male kings. She was honoured in death with two tombs – at both Giza and Abusir – and in the Giza tomb is depicted wearing the royal false beard and *uraeus*. It is likely that both served as regents for young sons.

BELOW: **The tomb of Khentkawes I, called in an inscription 'the mother of two kings'. Her extraordinary tomb was cut into a cube of bedrock; the stone around it was quarried for nearby pyramids. Khentkawes was probably the last member of the Fourth Dynasty to be buried at Giza.**

Instead of giving administrative positions to their own sons, the kings of this period sought new methods to maintain their supremacy. An important tool to secure loyalty was to marry royal daughters to top officials; another means was to focus worship especially of the sun god Ra in royal hands. We have already seen that kings had claimed the title 'son of Ra'; six of the first seven rulers of the new dynasty constructed major temples of Ra. The better-preserved of the two sun temples at Abu Gurab was constructed by Nyuserra and shows how much rulers invested in this newly prominent deity. The Abu Gurab temple is a major edifice carved with important reliefs. But investigators have noted that the carving was on poor-quality stone, smartened up with lime plaster coating. Perhaps the lower quality of this work is evidence of economic strain as rulers stretched resources to build both temples and pyramids simultaneously. More properly speaking, the pharaohs continued to invest a great many resources in pyramid *complexes*: the pyramids themselves were more modest than those of the Fourth Dynasty,

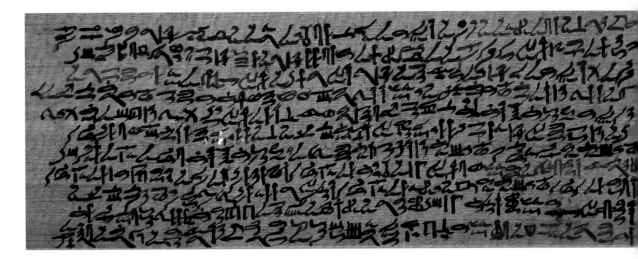

but the symbolic role of the surrounding buildings was enhanced, including much more relief carving.

The message royal building projects were intended to convey was always the divine stature of the king. Texts from this period tell specifically that the god Osiris was the first king of Egypt. They go beyond that, however, to explicitly identify the dead kings, buried in their pyramids, with Osiris himself. Such an identification was probably made earlier, but more extensive texts from this period allow us to see royal ideology more clearly. Crucial evidence is provided by the Pyramid Texts. Starting with Unas, last king of the Fifth Dynasty, the walls of the antechamber and royal burial chamber were inscribed with long columns of hieroglyphs, spells to help guide the soul of the dead pharaoh to the afterlife.

Also vital to understanding the ideology of kingship is *The Maxims of Ptahhotep*, an early work of 'wisdom literature' written in the Fifth Dynasty. The work emphasizes the spirit of *maat*, holding up righteous behaviour, care for the poor and oppressed, kindness and respect as the highest virtues. The text is a window into the world as it ought to be, the world that it was the pharaohs' highest duty to preserve and restore if necessary. While all kings must to some extent have demonstrated adherence to *maat* in their lives or actions, we can see it at work most clearly in the rule of Userkaf, who founded new settlements, especially in Lower Egypt, as a demonstration of royal restoration of *maat*. Userkaf, like other pharaohs, also saw to the establishment and refurbishment of provincial temples.

Trade and mining were big business under the Fifth Dynasty kings. Sahura was particularly active in this regard. He was the first to send fleets along the Palestine coast, launching military operations in southern Palestine as well as trading, and also dispatched expeditions to Punt. Most strikingly, in his reign

ABOVE: Only one complete copy of the *Maxims of Ptahhotep* survives, the version written on the Papyrus Prisse, now in the Bibliothèque Nationale in Paris. It was found in a tomb of the Seventeenth Dynasty.

the copper mines of Sinai were exploited on an immense scale. An inscription of Sahura has been found at Wadi el-Kharif, where 200 furnaces were erected to process the ore of the great copper mines. The recent discovery of a vast complex of 3,000–4,000 smelting units at Seh Nasb probably dates to about the same period.

CHALLENGES TO POWER IN THE SIXTH DYNASTY (2345–2181 BC)

By the time the Sixth Dynasty rose to power, cracks were appearing in the facade of royal power and divine majesty. Teti, the first pharaoh of the new dynasty, was not his predecessor's son, although he married Princess Iput to

A KING'S VOICE

It is only at the end of the Old Kingdom that we can finally get a glimpse of a living, breathing Egyptian king. The evidence comes from the tomb of Harkhuf, governor of Aswan. Harkhuf went south on an expedition when Pepy II was still a boy, and on his journey acquired a pygmy. The governor immediately informed the king, and Pepy responded with a letter in which we can still hear the excitement of a boy anxious

to receive a special gift. Pepy was eager to see the pygmy, he wrote, and gave extensive orders to protect the rarity. Harkhuf was to place guards around the unnamed pygmy to make sure he did not fall off the boat as he was brought downriver, he was to be fed the best food, men were to sleep around him and make sure he was well in the night, and so on. Harkhuf was so flattered by this mark of personal royal attention that he inscribed the whole letter on the wall of his tomb.

LEFT: **Governor Harkhuf of Upper Egypt, who served Merenra and Pepy II, shown here in a relief in his tomb, which was discovered at Qubbet el-Hawa. The autobiography of Harkhuf is an invaluable source for Egyptian dealings with the south at the end of the Old Kingdom.**

tap into the royal bloodline. Teti's Horus name, 'pacifier of the Two Lands', suggests some civil strife. Other ominous signs appear in his reign, notably that in several noble tombs of the time the original owner's name was erased and the king bestowed the tomb on a different official, suggesting that the king had to deal with opposition in his own court. Worst of all, an admittedly late tradition reports that Teti was murdered by his own bodyguard.

Queen Iput then served as regent for her young son Pepy I, but the myth of divine kingship had been severely dented. When Pepy came of age, he took seven or eight wives, perhaps contracting too many political marriages and thus allowing the rise of interest groups at court. One of those wives, Weret-

OPPOSITE: **Alabaster statue of Ankhesenmeryre II holding her son, the child king Pepy II. The queen mother probably served as regent for Pepy, who came to the throne when he was only six years old.**

Especially the second half of Pepy II's reign was a time of declining state power, as long-term royal policies ended by weakening the monarchy itself.

Imtes, eventually plotted against Pepy. We have only a tantalizing hint that this harem plot ever occurred. A courtier named Weni included in his tomb autobiography that there was a judicial issue in the royal women's quarters – a secret charge was brought against the queen that only he was considered worthy to judge. Most likely, Weret-Imtes was trying to secure the succession for her son. A late story reported by Herodotus tells that another unnamed ruler of the Old Kingdom, perhaps Merenra II, was murdered in a large-scale plot. Nitocris, the king's sister-wife, took revenge by assembling hundreds of officials for a feast in a subterranean room and then flooding it. Herodotus says that Nitocris went on to rule for a year, finally killing herself by leaping into a room filled with ashes. Modern Egyptologists doubt her existence.

The last significant ruler of the Old Kingdom was Pepy II. He came to the throne at the age of six; Manetho reports that the king ruled for 94 years, although about 60 years is more likely. Especially the second half of Pepy II's reign was a time of declining state power, as long-term royal policies ended by weakening the monarchy itself. Kings had massively endowed temples and their own mortuary complexes, exempting many from taxes and labour service and ultimately weakening their economic power so much that Pepy was unable to perform his designated role. Without a strong hand to control them, the local governors (nomarchs) claimed much more independence and their offices became hereditary, even as the king showered wealth on them, depleting the royal treasury to buy their loyalty. Next to nothing is known of Pepy II's successor Nitiqret (most Egyptologists believe this was a male king, not Herodotus' Nitocris), and for over a century strong rule by sons of Ra, governing a unified Egypt, became an increasingly distant memory.

ROYAL DECLINE & RECOVERY

Historians disagree on when the Old Kingdom ended. Whether one reckons the end of an era with the last ruler of the Sixth Dynasty or also includes the ephemeral kings of the Seventh and Eighth Dynasties (2181–2160 BC), though, it is clear that the Egyptian monarchy faced trying times after the death of the long-lived Pepy II in 2184 BC. What followed is known as the First Intermediate Period (2160–2055 BC). Later eras regarded it as a time of crisis and calamity, the lack of a single accepted pharaoh meaning that the forces of chaos could reign freely. The whole period was interpreted – after the fact – to support the ideology of kingship, writers in the later Middle Kingdom assuming that without a strong king Egypt could not possibly have prospered. Perhaps no greater condemnation of the era exists than that the Saqqara King List leaves the rulers of the First Intermediate Period out completely, trying to create the impression of a seamless transition from the Old Kingdom to the Middle Kingdom.

OPPOSITE: **One of seven granite sphinxes of Amenemhat III. Joining the lion's strength with human intelligence, the sphinx was a popular royal symbol. These statues were moved to Tanis in c. 1000 BC by Psusennes I, who added the hieroglyphic inscription between the figure's paws.**

RIGHT: **Scarab of Amenemhat III. Scarabs – beetle-shaped amulets and seals – were popular throughout ancient Egypt, and often provide valuable clues about the pharaohs.**

THE EROSION OF EGYPTIAN KINGSHIP IN THE FIRST INTERMEDIATE PERIOD

The reality was more complicated. To start, it is hard, at a distance of more than 4,000 years, even to ascertain whether there was a crisis in the material well-being of the Egyptians. The argument has been made that Egypt suffered in the megadrought that devastated western Asia in the late 3rd millennium BC, lower Nile inundations leading to widespread famine and erosion of the tax base. But the evidence that what is known as the '4.2 kiloyear megadrought' had an impact on Egypt is far from clear, and in fact urban centres were flourishing at the end of the Old Kingdom, making it unlikely that Egypt suffered a subsistence crisis. The majority of scholars now believe that the First Intermediate Period was not so much a period of decline as it was an era in which wealth, and thus power, were redistributed.

That redistribution had a highly negative effect on the monarchy. Royal wealth decreased, perhaps thanks to the cumulative effect of too many tax exemptions, and with it the ability of the monarchy to act declined until, by the end of the Eighth Dynasty in 2160 BC, Upper and Lower Egypt had completely separated governmentally, with a number of regional elites setting up as independent rulers. While the institutions of government continued in the Seventh and Eighth Dynasties, they operated on a reduced scale, for example the royal distribution centres (*hut*) significantly declining. More generally, the position the pharaohs had held as the source of all wealth eroded; in the First Intermediate Period there is much more evidence of people inheriting assets or acquiring riches by their own efforts, rather than as gifts from pharaoh. The trade networks of the Old Kingdom continued to operate, but at least sometimes they were controlled by nomadic groups and a rising Egyptian 'middle class' rather than by the state.

BELOW: **The Saqqara Tablet, a king list from the New Kingdom, lists the rulers of Egypt from the First Dynasty to Rameses II of the Nineteenth Dynasty. Although partially destroyed, the inscription has helped scholars reconstruct the chronology of early Egypt.**

We can see the erosion of Egyptian kingship in the growing pretension of the noble class as well. By the Sixth Dynasty, important administrators through the country were erecting monumental tombs for themselves. Especially impressive were the funerary arrangements of the nomarchs, the regional governors who acted with increasing independence and succeeded in making their offices hereditary. Strikingly, these nomarchs, in the boastful autobiographies they had carved on the walls of their burial chambers, claimed a protective role that had traditionally belonged to the king. For example, the nomarch Ankhtify brags that he fed many towns in a famine (a famine that may not even have existed, since Ankhtify's contemporary Iti claims to have fed Ankhtify's own capital city at the same time), presenting himself as the 'great chieftain' caring for his society. Ankhtify did include a mention of King Kaneferre of the Ninth Dynasty (*c.*2160–*c.*2130 BC), but the pharaoh is marginalized in the text while Ankhtify himself claims to be 'unequalled'. There is, to be sure, a new emphasis on civil war or famine in these autobiographies, and it is unlikely that *all* the reports were just literary *topoi* – but the local noble always claims that he successfully overcame the obstacles presented. By contrast, there is a glaring gap in royal monuments during the First Intermediate Period, demonstrating that the central institutions of the state were no longer functioning.

After the death of Pepy II, pharaohs continued to rule a united Egypt in

the Seventh and Eighth Dynasties, but administration rapidly became less complex. There was certainly an extended succession crisis at the end of the Old Kingdom, perhaps caused in large part because Pepy II had too many sons, grandsons and even great-grandsons all vying for power at the same time. Manetho reports that the Seventh Dynasty consisted of 70 kings who reigned for a grand total of 70 days; while these numbers are doubtless symbolic, modern Egyptologists have found evidence of at least five pharaohs who claimed the throne within the course of a year. All were probably related to Pepy II, and at least four of his sons were kings in the Eighth Dynasty, which produced a rather more moderate 27 kings in 146 years. Almost the only physical remains of this vast assembly of rulers are a small pyramid constructed for Qakare Ibi of the Eighth Dynasty and a very few of his artefacts.

The pharaohs of the Eighth Dynasty claimed to govern Egypt from Memphis, but probably just controlled the area around that city, central weakness leading to a confused period with various families exerting their authority over various regions. Meanwhile, with the end of clear royal control, Egypt lost territory in both the north and the south. Peoples from western Asia, probably nomadic 'sand-dwellers', overran at least the northern part of the Delta. We can see the shift of power in favour of the nomads as early as the reign of Pepy II, who had to send an expedition to recover the bodies of Egyptians the nomads had killed. Even more dire for royal finances, the rulers

OPPOSITE: **Ankhtify's tomb at el-Mo'alla is one of the best preserved from the First Intermediate Period. The walls are covered with scenes of peaceful agricultural life, as in this detail.**

LEFT: **Fragment of a relief depicting a group of Nubian mercenaries. Employment of Nubian fighters had become common by the end of the Old Kingdom; they were especially famed as bowmen.**

BELOW: A number of kings of the Ninth and Tenth Dynasties were named Khety; they ruled the area around Herakleopolis. This limestone statue depicts one of these largely unknown rulers.

With the end of clear royal control, Egypt lost territory in both the north and the south.

of this period lost control of the trade routes that stretched into Nubia. The Sixth Dynasty had maintained garrisons as far south as the fortress of Defula near the third cataract, and Merenra had even ordered the cutting of five canals at the cataracts to ease ship traffic upriver. All this was lost as the First Intermediate Period stretched on.

Another sign of weakening royal power is that kings increasingly relied on mercenary Nubian and Libyan troops for their military ventures, perhaps because they were unable to secure the services of their own subjects.

HERAKLEOPOLITAN RULERS OF THE NINTH AND TENTH DYNASTIES (2160–2055 BC)

The rulers of the Ninth and Tenth Dynasties were of royal stock and regarded themselves as the heirs of the Old Kingdom; one was even buried in the royal necropolis at Saqqara (in an admittedly small pyramid). Their power was quite limited, however. The kings moved the capital from Memphis to Henen-nesw, which was renamed Herakleopolis in the Ptolemaic period, when Greeks identified the local god with the hero Herakles. These Herakleopolitan rulers are largely unknown, since most did not last very long on the throne and because excavation in northern Egypt is much more limited thanks to the height of the current water table. Most of what we know about these dynasties comes from private tombs. The founder of the dynasty, Khety I, was probably nomarch of Herakleopolis before he seized the throne.

Although he claimed the title 'king of Upper and Lower Egypt', Khety never succeeded in controlling the land south of Abydos in anything but the most loose of overlordships. Khety left an evil reputation. Manetho reports that this would-be unifier was 'more terrible than his predecessors' and was noted for his brutality. Always fond of moralizing tales, this late historian relates that the gods drove the tyrant mad and Khety met his end when he was eaten by a crocodile. While we have no means of uncovering the truth of the story, Khety I does appear to have died relatively young;

BELOW: A number of kings of the Ninth and Tenth Dynasties were named Khety; they ruled the area around Herakleopolis. This limestone statue depicts one of these largely unknown rulers.

TALE OF THE ELOQUENT PEASANT

The Middle Kingdom produced a considerable quantity of 'pessimistic literature' – tales, admonitions and even pseudo-prophecy – that paint a dark picture of Egypt during the First Intermediate Period. These works brand the era as a time of civil war, administrative breakdown and famine. For example, the *Complaints of Khakheperresonbe* portray a nation in deep distress and the author urges his own heart to show courage in the face of adversity. The *Admonitions of Ipuwer* tell of the evils of a state without a strong ruler and call for a strong king to restore *maat*. We should beware of just accepting such literary works at face value, however. All were produced well after a strong central government had been re-established, and were designed to tout how much better the author's own time is.

One of these works is the *Tale of the Eloquent Peasant*. The story, probably set in the reign of Khety II of the Ninth Dynasty, tells how a peasant named Khunianupu was taking his produce to market, only to have the son of a court official steal his laden donkeys and beat him. The local officials refused to help the hapless man, so Khunianupu complained to the royal steward – so eloquently that the steward told the king about it. The king ordered that the steward continue putting the peasant off, meanwhile writing down everything Khunianupu said for the king to read. So, day after day, the peasant complained, laying out in the process Egyptian beliefs about what a state should be – ruled by the principle of maat with a strong king who assures justice and prosperity for all. Finally, after reading the transcripts, the king punished the wrongdoer and the peasant was rewarded, besides having his goods restored.

At first sight a tale of a society in crisis, in which royal officials and their families are a law unto themselves, this story is at least in part a satire on the difficulties of working with the Egyptian bureaucracy. It also shows a pharaoh acting (eventually) as he ought, serving as the arbiter of justice. The king is also presented as benevolent, ordering that Khunianupu at court and the peasant's family back home be supplied with food, even as he turns an apparently deaf ear to the legal plaint. One should note, however, the layers of administration between peasant and ruler; the peasant is never actually admitted to pharaoh's presence. The lesson being taught is that the king is distant, but ultimately deeply concerned with justice and equity – in short, with the restoration of *maat*.

ABOVE: **Excerpt from the Ipuwer Papyrus, a text written in the simplified hieratic script during the Nineteenth Dynasty. It contains the *Admonitions of Ipuwer*, one of the most important literary works of the Twelfth Dynasty.**

Khety II's mother served as regent for the first four years of his reign, so he was only a boy when his father died.

THE NOMARCHS OF THEBES

While the Ninth and Tenth Dynasties ruled from Herakleopolis, the nomarchs of Thebes established themselves as the leading power in Upper Egypt; their adoption of royal titles marks the beginning of the Eleventh Dynasty (2125–2055 BC). Dynasties Ten and Eleven ruled as rivals, one holding the north and the other the south, for about 30 years. The Herakleopolitan ruler eventually provoked a crisis, however. Allies of the northern ruler assaulted the south and got out of hand, desecrating temples and even the royal tombs. The reaction against this blatant sacrilege allowed the Theban king to pull his people together for what amounted to a holy war against the Herakleopolitans, leading in time to reunification.

BELOW: **Nobles, like kings, were happy to depict scenes of daily life in their tombs. In this fragment of a limestone stela, Intef son of Henyt and his wife Dedetamun enjoy the food offerings their son has brought them. The stela dates to the Twelfth Dynasty.**

By the time Mentuhotep II became pharaoh of a newly united Egypt in
c.2040 BC, Thebes and its kings had accomplished an impressive consolidation
of power. In the Old Kingdom, Thebes (ancient Waset) had been a minor
provincial capital, but a nomarch named Intef had built up his independent
authority, and Intef's successor Mentuhotep I was bold enough to call himself a
king, at least posthumously. His son Intef I at first called himself 'supreme chief
of Upper Egypt', but eventually took a Horus name, thus declaring himself king,
after conquering the rival cities of Koptos, Dendera and Hierakonpolis. Intef's
Horus name – 'pacifier of the Two Lands' – was unfortunately
just wishful thinking. His pretensions can
also be seen in the immense tomb

Although the bodies were not mummified, they were all placed in shrouds marked with the seal and cartouche of Mentuhotep II, marking the dead as pharaoh's comrades in arms.

he had constructed for himself, a sunken burial that called for the excavation of 400,00 cubic metres (14,125,870 cubic feet) of gravel and rock.

It was the reign of the third Theban king, Intef II, however, that was decisive. In his 50 years on the throne, Intef II claimed kingship over Lower as well as Upper Egypt and began making the wish into reality by capturing the nome (province) of Abydos to the north of Thebes. The Theban ruler had sufficient resources and notions of appropriate royal behaviour to import produce and regulate its distribution during a famine. Intef II also declared himself to be 'son of Ra' and added a Horus name – although not the full five-fold titulary of Old Kingdom monarchs – to his birth name. A stele outside Intef II's tomb described his conquests, and in a rare human moment the pharaoh chose to be depicted with his five dogs, the name of each carefully inscribed on the monument.

BELOW: Funerary stela of Intef II, who ruled much of Upper Egypt in the Eleventh Dynasty. Intef's reign of nearly 50 years laid the foundation for Thebes' reunification of Egypt.

THE DAWN OF THE MIDDLE KINGDOM (2055–1650 BC)

Intef III continued to expand the territory under his sway, but the final push to reunification came in the reign of Mentuhotep II. Drawing Egypt together under a single king must have involved much negotiation; we can see hints of that in Mentuhotep's marriage to Neferu-Khayet, heiress of the Elephantine nome. But there was also violent warfare, with troops at least sometimes led by the pharaoh in person. Hierakonpolis itself was captured, and the tombs of the Herakleopolitan rulers purposely desecrated; Merykara, the last Herakleopolitan king, had died

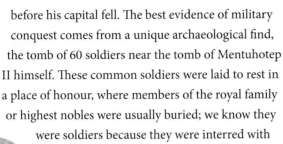

before his capital fell. The best evidence of military conquest comes from a unique archaeological find, the tomb of 60 soldiers near the tomb of Mentuhotep II himself. These common soldiers were laid to rest in a place of honour, where members of the royal family or highest nobles were usually buried; we know they were soldiers because they were interred with their weapons. From the location of their wounds, forensic scientists have determined that these men were killed in an assault on a fortified place. Some were killed outright by blows from above, while others were wounded and then clubbed to death by defenders. Their bodies then lay on the field long enough for scavenger birds to start their work but, rather later, clearly after a successful final assault, they were brought back to Thebes for burial. Although the bodies were not mummified, they were all placed in shrouds marked with the seal and cartouche of Mentuhotep II, marking the dead as pharaoh's comrades in arms. They had probably died in the final battle of a long campaign.

We can see the phases of reunification in the changes Mentuhotep made to his titles. Sometime after the 14th year of his reign in Thebes, the king changed his Horus name and added a Two Ladies name. Then, in Year 39, he assumed the Horus name 'he who united the two countries' (*Smatowy*) and added a Golden Falcon name.

Mentuhotep II's conquest marks the dawn of the Middle Kingdom, with a vigorous restatement of the monarch's position as god, mediator with the gods and protector of Egypt. His reunification was recognized as a great achievement, celebrated as late as the Twentieth Dynasty (1186–1069 BC). Try as they might, however, the pharaohs of the Middle Kingdom could not replicate the conditions of the Old Kingdom, and probably did not attempt to do so. In the reconstituted Egypt, kings no longer

LEFT: One of 22 statues of Mentuhotep II that originally lined the path to his mortuary complex at Deir el-Bahri. Purposely crafted in archaic style, they show the great unifier wearing the crown of Lower Egypt and the traditional garment of the sed festival. The hands would originally have held the crook and flail of kingship.

had a monopoly on foreign trade, and also failed to restore the efficient tax system of the earliest kings. Pharaohs also opted not to rebuild the network of royal distribution centres that had been a hallmark of the Old Kingdom. Their age had passed, with the development of a more market-driven economy and nascent middle class.

BELOW: Henenu was the steward of Mentuhotep III in _c._2000 BC. In his tomb autobiography he tells of leading a 3,000-man expedition to reopen trade to the south. Henenu was buried at Deir el-Bahri.

Mentuhotep's new beginning was impressive. A high priority was to curb the power of provincial nomarchs, so Mentuhotep created a system of circuit officials, sent regularly from the court to inspect and regulate the nomarchs. At some point in his reign, the pharaoh was secure enough to start sending expeditions into Nubia; his troops pushed as far south as the second cataract. He also dispatched a series of expeditions to collect building materials, including one led by the steward Henenu, who took 3,000 soldiers as well as other troops to clear 'rebels' from the road; Henenu boasted that his men dug 12 wells along their route. Large

quantities of stone were needed, both to restore temples up and down the Nile and for Mentuhotep II's own huge funerary temple at Deir el-Bahri. Little of the edifice still survives, but what remains demonstrates the ruler's programme of self-deification, already visible in his second Horus name – 'the divine one of the white crown'. He was depicted as a god in company with the gods, named himself son of the goddess Hathor and usurped some of the insignia of the major gods Amun and Min. A processional axis connected the mortuary temple to Karnak, thus linking Amun to the king who was buried at Deir el-Bahri.

MENTUHOTEP'S SUCCESSORS

The path of the late Eleventh Dynasty did not run smoothly, however. There were accomplishments, such as the foundation of the harbour town of Kuser on the Red Sea to serve as a base for trade expeditions to Punt. But when Mentuhotep III died in 1992 BC, his successor Mentuhotep IV may not even have been a member of the royal family, but rather a usurper. He was not included on the king lists; instead there is a report of 'seven empty years'. We only know about him from inscriptions that commemorate quarrying expeditions. One of these, led by the royal vizier Amenemhat, was on a massive scale. Ten thousand men were sent to Wadi Hammamat to procure a block of stone that could serve as a lid for the king's sarcophagus. We are told that they were led to the perfect rock for the purpose by a pregnant gazelle, who gave birth on the stone itself.

Vizier Amenemhat was probably the same man who, shortly after the expedition, became founder of the Twelfth Dynasty (1985–1773 BC). It is not clear if he seized the throne in a coup or was named as Mentuhotep IV's successor. There are some signs of disorder in Egypt at the time, including graffiti found at Hatnub that describe civil war conditions in Middle Egypt. The Horus name Amenemhat I adopted – 'he who calms the heart of the two

ABOVE: **This lintel comes from Amenemhat I's mortuary temple at Lisht. It depicts the pharaoh celebrating the** *sed* **festival. Two gods particularly associated with coronations, Horus and Anubis, stand on either side, offering Amenemhat an ankh, the symbol for life. Nekhbet and Wadjet, the patron deities of Upper and Lower Egypt, complete the composition.**

OVERLEAF: **Amenemhat I's pyramid at Lisht. Although originally comparable in size to the great pyramids, less durable construction methods have reduced Amenemhat's tomb to only about 20m (65ft) tall. The pyramid's interior passages have never been explored; they are below the current water table.**

THE HUMAN FACE OF PHARAOH

In the Middle Kingdom, writers and artists, while continuing to portray the king's divine stature, also took pains to stress his humanity. In *The Instruction of Amenemhat*, for instance, the text pulses with the king's disappointment and disillusionment as the ghost of Amenemhat describes his own murder. While presented as in some ways more than a mere mortal – the ghost complains that if he had not been caught by surprise and weaponless he would have defeated the guards who slaughtered him – the very fact that a pharaoh's assassination should have been described in detail suggests a new willingness to engage with the monarch's mortality. Art, especially from the time of Senusret III and later, also displays a new realism. Representations of Old Kingdom kings are idealized and godlike, showing no emotion and intended to radiate a sense of strength. The statuary of Middle Kingdom rulers, by contrast, presents us with lined, tired faces, presenting pharaohs who were clearly weighed down by the burdens of their high office.

Literature sometimes even made fun of pharaohs. It was a Middle Kingdom author who described a bored pharaoh deciding to amuse himself by being rowed on a lake by young women of the court wearing only fishnets – a charming, lifelike scene, but hardly one that emphasizes pharaoh's role as living god. Perhaps the most extraordinary tale of the Middle Kingdom presents the

lands' – also suggests that his ascension was preceded by political instability. Amenemhat was the son of commoners; his father Senusret is simply named as 'god's father' and his mother Nefret as 'king's mother' in inscriptions. Another sign of the irregularity of Amenemhat's succession is that it was given after-the-fact divine approval in the form of a propagandistic pseudo-prophetic text, the *Words of Neferty*, which was probably composed early in the Twelfth Dynasty. Purporting to come from an earlier time, the text tells of a coming time of destruction, when Asiatics will invade and even the Nile will run dry, while the great will be reduced to beggary and the poor will be enriched. A king, evocatively named 'Ameny', will come from the south, the son of a Nubian woman. This man, a thinly disguised Amenemhat I, will unite the two lands and drive out chaos.

Amenemhat I proved to be a strong ruler. He established a new capital, which he named Amenemhat Itjtawy – 'Amenemhat, seizer of the two lands'. The site of Itjtawy has not yet been discovered, but it was probably near the Twelfth Dynasty's necropolis at Lisht, right at the border between Upper and Lower Egypt. We can see the new dynasty's aspiration to emulate the pharaohs

Old Kingdom's King Pepy II in a far from flattering light, so human that his divine nature vanishes completely. According to this tale, Pepy had a gay lover, an army commander (despite the fact that ancient Egyptian cultural norms strongly condemned homosexuality). Unable to admit publicly to the relationship, instead Pepy snuck out of the palace alone at night for a lover's tryst. Such tales certainly suggest that some of the godlike lustre had evaporated from the person of the pharaoh.

RIGHT: Papyrus was expensive, so it was common for Egyptians to write on ostraka, broken pieces of pottery. This ostrakon was inscribed with part of *The Instruction of Amenemhat*.

of the Old Kingdom in the pyramid Amenemhat had constructed at Lisht. It was of impressive size, with a base 116.4m (282ft) wide and a height of 54.9m (180ft). It was not up to the standard of the great pyramids, however; constructed of poor-quality stone, blocks pilfered from other sites, and mudbrick, it is now a jumbled pile that stands at a height of 19.8m (65ft).

Besides proving that he could marshal the resources to construct a new town and a pyramid, Amenemhat was also responsible for the Wall of the Prince, a series of fortresses placed to protect the kingdom's eastern and western borders. He campaigned against both Asiatics and Nubians, and vigorously suppressed nomarchs inclined to be too independent. It is possible that Amenemhat also added stability by naming his son Senusret as co-ruler; certainly some rulers of the Twelfth Dynasty shared their throne in that way.

Although he moved his chief residence to Itjtawy, Amenemhat I remained a loyal son of Thebes, especially by promoting the cult of Amun, Thebes' chief deity. He may have been responsible for the original shrine of Amun at Karnak. Karnak, over the course of the following two millennia, became

ABOVE: Part of the enormous temple complex at Karnak, dedicated to the god Amun. Starting in the Middle Kingdom, for over 2,000 years pharaohs added shrines, colonnades and statuary to honour the greatest of the gods.

OPPOSITE: Sandstone statue of Senusret I, depicted as Osiris. This is one of six statues of the king found at the outer enclosure wall of his mortuary complex at Lisht.

a massive religious complex covering 1 sq km (250 acres), a dense forest of temples, shrines, obelisks, columns and statues. The importance of Thebes for the rest of Egyptian history was thus assured.

All was not well, though. Amenemhat I's 30-year reign ended in violence, a coup attempt in which pharaoh himself was murdered. We have a surprisingly personal and moving account of the assassination, probably composed by the scribe Aktoy in the reign of Amenemhat's successor Senusret I. This text, *The Instruction of Amenemhat*, tells of the late king's ghost coming in a dream to Senusret and giving him sage advice, including an admonition to trust no one and have no intimates. The ghost mourns that somebody he had trusted and favoured plotted against him. As he lay resting after dinner one day, members of his own guard burst into the chamber. Roused from sleep and with no weapons to hand, the king fell to their blades. If the plot had intended to put a more junior prince on the throne it failed, however, and Senusret I soon established himself as the new king.

CONSOLIDATION AND EXPANSION
IN THE TWELFTH DYNASTY

The seven kings and one queen who constituted the Twelfth Dynasty presided over a period of Egyptian consolidation and expansion for 210 years. The pharaohs' ability to assert their authority in the provinces gradually rose, and they established control over individuals and their duties to the government that was probably even greater than what the Old Kingdom rulers had enjoyed. They took steps to curb the nomarchs, and in fact town mayors became more central to the kingdom's administration than the provincial governors. All the rulers of the Middle Kingdom kept annals, and although only fragments have survived, they tell of a central preoccupation with building, refurbishing and donating to temples, thus visibly presenting themselves – and courting the priesthoods – throughout the land. The fragmentary annals of Amenemhat II also reinforce the image of royal life as a constant round of rituals.

In the reign of Senusret I, the process of recentralizing power in the king's hands proceeded apace. He appears to have had considerable success at keeping important resources out of the hands of the provincial elites, since nomarchs could no longer afford to construct monumental tombs for themselves. Senusret, by contrast, erected a full pyramid complex, following exactly the layout used in the Old Kingdom. In what became a new symbol of royal power and connection to the sun god Ra, Senusret also had two great obelisks erected to commemorate the *sed* festival with which he celebrated 30 years of rule. These obelisks, each carved from a single piece of red granite, standing 20.1m (66ft) tall and weighing 110 tonnes (121 tons) each, were placed at the temple of Ra in Heliopolis. One of them stands there still, a monument to Senusret's greatness and of his conscious policy to link himself to all of Egypt's major temples.

For all his accomplishments, Senusret I may have narrowly escaped his father's fate. A great famine in the 25th year of his reign probably increased internal tensions and led to a palace intrigue. Something happened that led not only to the dismissal of Senusret's vizier, a man named Intefiqer who had served him for decades, but to his being formally cursed. Intefiqer's image

was hacked from the wall of his mother's tomb at Thebes. Even more evident of personal animosity was that Intefiqer was included along with foreign enemies on execration texts from Senusret's time. These are texts written in hieratic on clay statuettes, pots or clay tablets, calling on the gods to curse pharaoh's enemies. The text was then smashed – a fate, it was hoped, that would also befall those whose names were inscribed on it.

Senusret I's most significant accomplishment was an expansion of Egyptian rule southwards into Nubia. In the First Intermediate Period, Egyptians had lost control of the trade posts and fortresses established in Lower Nubia during the Old Kingdom, and a strong indigenous state, the kingdom of Kush, had formed in Lower Nubia. Since Egyptian rulers wanted Lower Nubia's granite, amethyst and diorite, not to mention access to the gold and copper mines further up the Nile, Kush was a major obstacle. Following his father's lead, Senusret I pushed southwards, establishing at least 13 forts as far upriver as the second cataract. Old Kingdom rulers had been content to secure the trade routes; their successors of the Middle Kingdom apparently intended real conquest and rule. For example, the Twelfth Dynasty added major fortifications to the settlement at Buhen, which had been founded near the second cataract in the Old Kingdom to support Egyptian mining

RIGHT: **The Middle Kingdom fortress of Buhen, on the west bank of the Nile below the second cataract. Heavily fortified as part of Egypt's southern defence line, Egyptian troops were posted at Buhen for centuries. Buhen was covered by the waters of Lake Nasser when the Aswan High Dam was completed.**

OPPOSITE: **The obelisk of Senusret I, the oldest standing obelisk still in Egypt. It stands in the al-Masalla district of what in ancient times was known as Heliopolis. Standing 20m (67ft) tall, the obelisk was erected to celebrate Senusret's *sed* festival.**

expeditions. Senusret's fortresses moved Egypt's border 400km (250 miles) south of Aswan. After that time, Nubians who did not want Egyptian rule were routinely categorized as 'rebels', although control of the region remained a challenge. Senusret I's son Amenemhat II had to lead further military campaigns into Nubia. In fact, he had already been sent there as a prince, accompanying an expedition led by the nomarch of Beni Hasan, who tells in his tomb autobiography that the expedition went so well that 'the king's son praised god for me'.

Control of Nubia reached its height in the reign of Senusret III, a warrior king who campaigned in Nubia in Years 6, 8, 10, 16 and 19 of his reign and reinforced the system of fortresses. To facilitate trade, he also cleared and expanded a canal originally dug in the reign of Merenra to bypass the first cataract. It was perhaps at this time that the Egyptians also constructed a mud-surfaced slipway, over 4.8km (3 miles) long, to move boats past the worst rapids of the second cataract.

BELOW: **Diadem of Princess Sithathoriunet, daughter of Senusret II. When her tomb at Lahun was excavated in 1914, archaeologists found a niche with boxes of jewellery and beauty products that ancient robbers had overlooked.**

Both Amenemhat II and Senusret II had to face ongoing problems of nomarchs trying to claim too much independence.

Amenemhat II is also credited with the restoration of sea trade with the Levant, a commerce that expanded in the reign of his son Senusret II. Indeed, it is hard to separate the reigns of these two kings. While Egyptologists have argued for a number of co-regencies in the Twelfth Dynasty, the first certain case is Senusret II's rule alongside his father for the last three years of Amenemhat II's life. Both rulers had to face ongoing problems of nomarchs trying to claim too much independence; Senusret II is credited with breaking these regional governors' power decisively with crippling taxes and other exactions. He was likely helped by a commanding physical appearance, standing 1.98m (6.5ft) tall.

BELOW: This pectoral represents pharaoh – in the form of a lion with the head of a hawk – trampling on Egypt's foes. It was found in the tomb of Princess Mereret at Dahshur; she may have been the daughter of Senusret III.

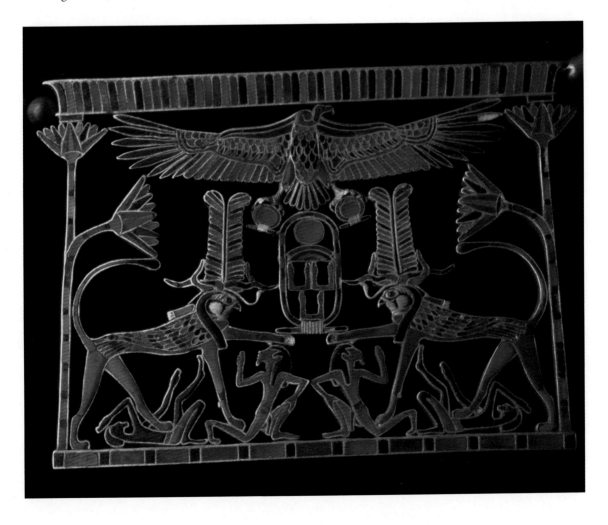

THE GREAT FAIYUM RECLAMATION SCHEME

It was probably Senusret II, Amenemhat II's successor, who began the great Faiyum reclamation scheme, a centrepiece of Middle Kingdom rule, although the scheme may have originated with his father. The Faiyum was a large region of rich marshland in central Egypt. In a project practically unique for the age, successive pharaohs constructed an extensive network of dykes and canals connecting the Faiyum with the waterway now called Bahr Yusuf. In the process, some of the water that would have flowed from the Nile into Lake Moeris was siphoned off, thus making the lake recede and opening up thousands of acres of rich farmland. The early interest in the region can be seen in Senusret II's decision to site his pyramid at Lahun, the entrance to the Faiyum, where two ancient dykes met. Amenemhat III continued the work of land reclamation, taking advantage of a period of economic growth and peace to construct a great wall, about 43.5km (27 miles) long, to hold back Lake Moeris and open up nearly 68.8 sq km (17,000 acres) for farming. Since the new land was claimed by the crown, the Faiyum became a major source of royal revenue.

EXPANSION AND BUREAUCRATIZATION

Senusret III, who succeeded his father in 1870 BC, continued both the process of enhancing trade with the Levant and the suppression of the nomarchs. No longer content merely to trade, Senusret intervened militarily in the northern Levant, taking control of Byblos, Egypt's long-time trading partner. After this time, Byblos no longer had a king, but only a 'mayor'. Clearly, nothing was to stand in the way of the Egyptian pharaoh's supremacy. This decisive intervention in western Asia was a new departure for Egypt's kings, giving birth to a legend reported by Herodotus that Senusret led troops as far as India. The intervention in Byblos was probably inspired by the same philosophy of rule that led Senusret III to divide Egypt into three administrative districts – Lower Egypt, Upper Egypt and Lower Nubia – each under the charge of a vizier and council. Senusret's goal appears to have been to reduce the authority of the nomarchs, although it is not clear how he succeeded in implementing this new plan. From this time, members of powerful regional families joined the royal bureaucracy, as can be seen by their choice to be buried near the capital rather than in their provinces.

OPPOSITE: **Colossal statue of Senusret III, found in the temple of Amun at Karnak. As is usual in art, the pharaoh is presented as an ideal physical specimen.**

POLITICAL AND ECONOMIC DECLINE

The Twelfth Dynasty reached its height – and began its decline – in the long reign of Amenemhat III. Amenemhat was the last major pyramid-builder. In fact, not content with a single pyramid, Amenemhat commissioned two.

Herodotus says Amenemhat III's mortuary temple complex was simply beyond description, and must have cost more in labour and money than all the public works in Greece combined.

The king was not buried in the Black Pyramid, constructed at Dahshur. It was a large edifice, but not very well built. Its mudbrick construction with limestone casing began to collapse, although not before two of Amenemhat's queens had been interred in a separate chamber within it. At first the pyramid was shored up, but then was abandoned in favour of a new tomb at Hawara in the Faiyum. Although also built of mudbrick with a limestone facing, the Hawara pyramid was not as tall, the architect seeking to relieve stress on the foundation. When the archaeologist Flinders Petrie explored its interior in 1889 he found the burial chamber flooded. As always with pyramids, a large mortuary complex surrounded the actual tomb. Little of Amenemhat III's mortuary temple complex has survived, but it was so elaborate that the Greeks called it the labyrinth. Herodotus reports that it was simply beyond description, and must have cost more in labour and money than *all* the public works in Greece combined.

By the end of Amenemhat III's 45-year reign, though, political and economic decline had set in. Possibly the king had exhausted the economy with his massive building activity and extensive exploitation of mines and quarries, the problem exacerbated by a series of low Nile inundations and the resultant low crop yields. His successor was Amenemhat IV, probably his son. Amenemhat IV ruled for only nine years, perhaps because he was already elderly when he inherited. He left little mark on history, except by leaving his sister-queen Sobekneferu to govern Egypt in a period of growing crisis.

BELOW: **The pyramid of Amenemhat III at Hawara. The pharaoh's burial chamber was hollowed out of a single block of quartzite that weighed about 110 tons; it was then covered with three 45-ton quartzite slabs. Despite such efforts, the pyramid was robbed in antiquity.**

SOBEKNEFERU – THE FIRST REIGNING QUEEN

Sometimes pharaohs married their half- or full sisters, although the practice was not as ubiquitous as has often been thought. These sibling matches occurred most frequently at times when it was necessary to reinforce the status of the monarch, perhaps in imitation of the brother–sister pairings of the gods. If these sister-consorts had a role to play in government because of their exalted birth, it has left no historical trace; they were not even always the 'great wife' whose son would automatically be the heir apparent. Nonetheless, to be the daughter of a pharaoh conferred special status, and in the absence of an adult male ruler, a queen who was also of royal blood could fill the governmental vacuum.

Such was the case with Sobekneferu, the only queen regnant of the Middle Kingdom. Amenemhat IV does not appear to have had a son with her or any other consort; there is no reason to think that Sobekneferu only served as a regent while a boy was growing to adulthood. Instead, Sobekneferu simply assumed the throne when her brother-husband died in 1777 BC and ruled for four years in her own name. Since there is no record of any conflict, she was probably the only member of the family left. Sobekneferu was, plainly and simply, the pharaoh. She was the first royal woman in Egyptian history to name herself the 'female Horus' – she called herself 'the female Hawk, beloved of Ra'. As reigning queen, her administration also employed the full five-fold titulary that marked the unique status of the king.

ABOVE: This bust of a pharaoh, wearing the *nemes* headcloth and *uraeus*, is thought to represent Amenemhat IV. It was discovered in the Faiyum. The realistic face with overly large nose may be an actual portrait of the king.

Little is known of Sobekneferu's activities during her reign, but scholars have been fascinated by the way she chose to present herself. A first important point is that she opted to be identified on monuments with her father Amenemhat III rather than with her husband, strongly suggesting that her right to rule depended on her royal blood rather than marriage. She saw to the completion of the great mortuary temple of her father at Hawara, again suggesting not just filial piety but a conscious desire to associate herself with her father.

But how to present oneself as king, when all the symbolism of monarchy was masculine? Egypt simply was not equipped for female rule, so the straightforward solution was to present the ruler as masculine, whether that was biologically true or not. Scribes, whether out of policy or confusion, gave Sobekneferu both masculine and feminine titles. It cannot simply have been by accident, however, that artists, while consistently depicting Sobekneferu

THE LAST PYRAMIDS

Nowhere is the Twelfth Dynasty's desire to emulate the glories of the Old Kingdom as plain as in the return to pyramids as the preferred royal tomb. Amenemhat I and Senusret I both situated their pyramids at Lisht, about 48km (30 miles) south of modern Cairo. Senusret's mortuary complex is the better preserved. His pyramid was once 105m (344ft) wide at its base. Senusret did not, however, have the resources of a Khufu or Khafra at his disposal – or perhaps the techniques for building a pyramid for eternity had been lost. While his pyramid was built of limestone, only the casing consisted of properly cut blocks, laid over a roughly prepared rubble core. Once the finely cut limestone was removed for other uses, the remainder of the pyramid rapidly collapsed. Other pyramids, even more cheaply constructed with a limestone facing over mudbrick, fared even worse, for example Amenemhat III's pyramid at Dahshur, now reduced to an eroded great lump of material.

The pharaohs of the Twelfth Dynasty continued to demand labour services from their subjects to build pyramids as well as

other tasks. Perhaps it is simply that more written material has survived from the Middle Kingdom, but the overwhelming impression is that this corvée (unpaid, forced) labour had become much more unpopular. Interesting evidence has been found at the town Senusret II constructed by his pyramid complex at Lahum to house builders and the mortuary priests. The town itself was centrally planned, a walled settlement laid out on a square with straight, wide streets and central stone-lined drains. Simple three-room houses were designed for the labourers, with increasingly elaborate homes for more important people, complete with bathrooms, granaries and garden pools. The whole town could have housed about 5,000 people. A papyrus letter from Lahun is an appeal on behalf of a man named Sobekemhab, who had absconded from the pyramid-building work at Hawara. He had been imprisoned, and the letter writer was afraid that Sobekemhab would die from the rigours of his confinement. Clearly, corvée work was highly undesirable if a man would risk so severe a penalty for avoiding it.

The Black Pyramid of Amenemhat III at Dahshur. The pyramid was built on clay rather than bedrock and almost immediately began to sink, gradually crushing the burial chambers below it. Eventually it was abandoned, and the pharaoh buried in a new pyramid complex.

as a woman, showed her in a combination of female and male clothing; the ceremonial wear of a male pharaoh was simply too fraught with tradition and significance to abandon. And the queen regnant also assumed a great pharaonic prerogative – she had a pyramid built for herself at Mazghuna.

Although little survives of Sobekneferu's pyramid beyond the substructure, archaeologists have determined that the queen was never buried there. We simply don't know what became of her. There is no evidence of any sort of violence at the end of her reign, of a coup launched by Egyptians outraged at the notion of a female ruler. Indeed, there is no sign that her rule was unpopular at all.

Sobekneferu certainly ruled in difficult times. Famine and economic dislocation stalked Egypt, probably limiting the monarch's ability completely to control the ever-present forces of chaos. Most likely, Sobekneferu simply died of natural causes. Since she left no child to take the throne, the resulting vacuum in authority led to further weakening of the central state.

BELOW: **Statuette of Neferhotep I, who was probably the third pharaoh of the Thirteenth Dynasty. Found in the Faiyum, the work is now displayed in Bologna's Archaeological Museum.**

QUICK-FIRE SUCCESSION OF THE THIRTEENTH DYNASTY (1773–AFTER 1650 BC)

The succeeding Thirteenth Dynasty was only 'dynastic' in the loosest sense. There was a rapid turnover of rulers who did not come from a single family line; some of them were certainly commoners. They succeeded one another in increasingly rapid succession; 50 to 60 kings are attested in a period that spanned about 150 years. We know little about these individual rulers and their brief reigns. Scholars have theorized that there was a series of military takeovers, but there is little evidence to support that view. The only king of the period with a clear military link was Neferhotep I, whose prosperous reign lasted 11 years. Neferhotep was apparently a Theban, and on a monument named his grandfather as 'soldier of the town'. But if not a series of coups, there was certainly some rivalry for the throne: some of the Thirteenth Dynasty pharaohs had their names erased from their monuments, usually a sign that a successor wanted to erase their memory and perhaps even deny a predecessor a happy afterlife; some seem to have been denied burial in the tombs they had prepared for themselves.

Individual rulers were obscure, but the institution of kingship continued with remarkable stability. Egypt's bureaucracy and administration remained intact for most of the dynasty, and for some time kept control of Lower Nubia. And although monumental

ABOVE: 'The Finding of Moses' by Lawrence Alma-Tadema (1904). It was commissioned by a true Egyptophile, Sir John Aird, the engineer responsible for the first Aswan Dam.

building declined, showing that the rulers of this dynasty were not as strong or perhaps as grandiose as their predecessors, the central government continued to function from Itjtawy. We even have a unique window into life at court from the time of Sobekhotep II, thanks to a papyrus (Papyrus Bulaq 18) that details the daily rations issued at the palace over a period of 12 days. The document shows the relative importance of royal family members and other palace residents. Three inner divisions were maintained. The inmost was restricted to the royal family, personal servants and children of nobles or allies being educated at the king's expense. A second area was set aside for audiences and banquets, while the outer palace was home to the royal bureaucracy. In other words, even as crisis deepened, royal ceremonial and the special status of the pharaoh were maintained.

Yet crisis there was. Royal income was eaten away by a series of high Nile inundations and resulting famines; with decreased royal revenue, the throne was less able to control the more outlying provinces. Provincial governors increasingly tried to exploit the situation and gain independence. Another major income stream was threatened when Lower Nubia began to rebel in the reign of Sobekhotep IV and finally broke free completely. Most ominous of all, the evidence of royal rule in the north, the Delta, gradually vanishes. The late kings of the Thirteenth Dynasty, from the time of Neferhotep I onwards, lost control of Lower Egypt. Eventually, the last ruler of the dynasty, Ay, had to withdraw from Itjtawy, moving further south while a foreign dynasty, the Hyksos, tightened its hold on the north of the kingdom. Egypt was once again divided, and the ruler of the north was not even an Egyptian. The Second Intermediate Period (1650–1550 BC) had begun.

REIMAGINING EGYPT IN A WIDER WORLD

By the time Ay, the last pharaoh of the Thirteenth Dynasty, died in about the year 1650 BC, Egypt was united no longer and the institution of kingship had taken a severe beating. Large swathes of territory had broken free from central control, setting up their own kings and refusing to acknowledge any authority but their own. It was probably still during the Thirteenth Dynasty that an official named Nehesy claimed the crown as an independent ruler; although he controlled only the small city of Xois, Nehesy and his successors are counted as the Fourteenth Dynasty (1773–1650 BC). Other cities and provinces likely also broke free, although the fragmentary nature of our sources for the period probably disguises some of the governmental chaos.

OPPOSITE: Migrants from western Asia had been moving into Egypt for most of the Middle Kingdom. A famous relief from the tomb of the court official Khnumhotep II (Twelfth Dynasty) shows a group of these people, labelled as "Aamu", presenting themselves with gifts.

RIGHT: A scarab inscribed with the name of 'the King's Eldest Son Nehesy', from the Second Intermediate Period. He was probably a prince of the Fourteenth Dynasty.

ABOVE: **The myth of violent Hyksos conquest of Egypt was popularized by artists like Hermann Vogel, whose 'Invasion of the Hyksos' (c.1880) presents the west-Asian rulers of northern Egypt implausibly as savage African tribesmen.**

The fact that we know the names of over a hundred kings from the Second Intermediate Period, an era of Egyptian history that lasted only about a century, suggests that there were multiple people calling themselves pharaoh at any given time. Moreover, Nubia won its independence from Egypt. Most importantly for Egypt's long-term self-image, a new dynasty claimed the throne of Lower Egypt, if not of the whole country – a dynasty ruled by the foreign Hyksos. From the perspective of a centralized monarchy, this new Second Intermediate Period was a time of crisis and chaos indeed.

A WARPED PERSPECTIVE?

It is important, however, to recognize what great propaganda value this period of foreign rule over part of Egypt had for pharaohs of the New Kingdom that succeeded it. As ever with Egyptian history, one must remember the ideology of *maat*, the right order of the world that it was the central task of rulers to preserve against the forces of chaos. Since in time the Seventeenth Dynasty (c.1580–1550 BC), based in Thebes, drove out the Hyksos and reunited Egypt, their version of events won and was retained for posterity. For their purposes, the Second Intermediate Period was a time of anarchy and failure of *maat* and the Hyksos were not only foreign but positively evil. Ahmose, the pharaoh of the reconquest, was a hero on a par with Menes and Mentuhotep II, the other great unifiers of Egypt. It was that traditional picture of Hyksos rule that was

passed on to European civilizations by later writers such as Josephus, who
reports massive destruction and looting at Hyksos hands, a claim for which
no physical evidence in fact exists. Similarly, Manetho tells that a great Hyksos
conquest involved the burning of cities, razing of temples, massacres and mass
enslavement of the oppressed Egyptians. Manetho even names the penultimate
Hyksos ruler as Apophis – after the evil snake god, the embodiment of chaos –
rather than his actual name Apepi, doubtless drawing on New Kingdom sources
when he does so. Although the Hyksos monuments were purposely destroyed
after their rule ended, archaeologists have uncovered enough evidence to paint
a picture of the Second Intermediate Period that is very different indeed from
this dire portrayal of invasion and catastrophe.

AN INFLUX OF IMMIGRANTS

While Egypt had never existed in glorious isolation from the
rest of the world, in the Old and Middle Kingdoms its
monarchs had been able to control foreign interactions
with relative ease. As we have seen, from an early
age, the Egyptians were interested in luxury goods
from the Levant, but the culture of western Asia
could not rival that of Egypt. As Egypt moved
into the Middle Kingdom, however, the
geographical picture was shifting. Significant
states were being formed in the Near and
Middle East. Greater urbanization in the
region led to ever more specialization
in crafts the Egyptians found desirable
– and also to greater pressure on the
subsistence-level agricultural systems of
the Canaanites, Mitanni and other small
states. We have already seen that the
Middle Kingdom intervened militarily on
the eastern seaboard of the Mediterranean,
most notably establishing overlordship over
Byblos. The pharaohs also founded settlements
on the fringes of Egypt to urbanize new areas,
natural magnets for the peoples of the eastern
Mediterranean. What eventually became the most
important of these planned towns was Avaris (modern
Tell el-Dala) in the eastern Delta, founded by Amenemhat I.
We do not know if the pharaohs purposefully settled Asiatics

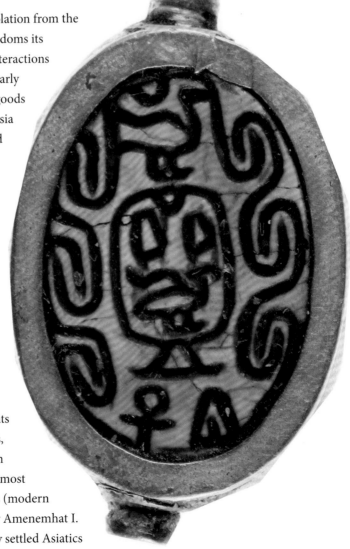

BELOW: **Scarab bearing
the name of the Hyksos
King Khayan, Fifteenth Dynasty
(*c.*1620–1581 BC).**

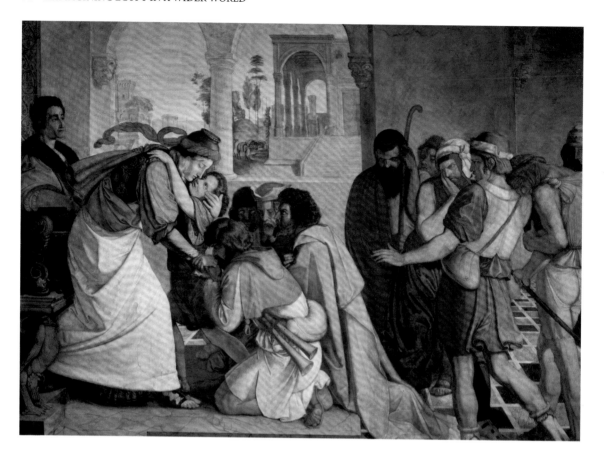

ABOVE: 'Joseph Reveals Himself to His Brothers', by Peter von Cornelius (1816). The origin of the biblical story of Joseph and the eventual exodus of the Hebrews from Egypt probably lies in the period of Hyksos rule, when the Hyksos welcomed western Asian migrants and gave them many important positions at their court.

at Avaris and other Delta sites or if they just came on their own in search of a better life. It is quite possible that they were established there purposefully at first, imported as experts in seafaring and other crafts the kings wished to exploit.

If what Egyptian sources call 'Asiatics' (mostly speakers of western Semitic languages) were brought purposely to Avaris, it was part of a general trend in the Middle Kingdom to open its doors to migrants. Egyptian texts and art constantly display contempt for the 'wretched Asiatics' and they were frequently named on the execration texts used to curse Egypt's enemies. In reality, however, more and more foreigners entered Egypt in the Middle Kingdom, and appear to have done so with the full knowledge and permission of the pharaohs. By late in the Middle Kingdom, some of these Asiatics held important positions at court, and some were certainly second-generation residents of Egypt; they are very visible in the sources by the reign of Amenemhat III. Other Asiatics entered Egypt as mercenaries or indentured servants; the kings allowed and perhaps encouraged large-scale migration in this way. The tale of Joseph and his brothers in Genesis, one of many families of Semites turning to Egypt for refuge during famines, is very believable. Still other Asiatics would have been introduced to

The pharaohs also founded settlements on the fringes of Egypt to urbanize new areas, which were natural magnets for the peoples of the eastern Mediterranean.

Egypt as slaves, captured in the wars that later Middle Kingdom rulers waged in Palestine. Senusret III in particular campaigned extensively in Palestine, and his monuments give him the proud title 'throat-slitter of the Asiatics'.

Even as Senusret wreaked havoc in Palestine, Avaris grew. It was a well-chosen site, close enough to the Mediterranean to serve as a harbour and a convenient starting point for overland routes to the Sinai, which Middle Kingdom rulers mined more and more extensively. Both Egyptians and Asiatics settled in Avaris, and extensive excavation of the site has revealed a great deal about the rising tide of immigration into the Delta. Much of the architecture at Avaris was Canaanite rather than Egyptian, and finds such as pottery vessels also display strong Canaanite influence. Yet archaeologists did not find ethnically defined districts; instead what developed in the city was a society of acculturated and partly acculturated Asiatics living side by side with native Egyptians. The foreigners had moved peacefully into the city, and were certainly not hostile to Egyptian cultural norms. Nor were Canaanites the only newcomers who settled in Avaris. Fragments of Minoan wall painting have been found on the site, including scenes of ancient Crete's famous bull leaping, suggesting that at least some Cretans had actually settled in the city as well, rather than just visiting occasionally to trade. Avaris swelled into one of the largest cities of the Near East, covering an area of about 642 acres (260 hectares) at its height.

BELOW: 'Osiris Beguiled into the Chest', an illustration from *The Myths of Ancient Egypt* by Lewis Spence (1917). The myth tells that Seth trapped his brother with a trick, then killed him and scattered his dismembered body over Egypt. Osiris' loyal wife Isis reassembled and reanimated her husband.

THE HYKSOS AT AVARIS

Rather than foreigners moving in and seizing control of the Delta by force, the picture emerges that the western Asians who settled in such large numbers at Avaris and other sites simply gradually started ruling themselves as the Thirteenth Dynasty's hold on power loosened. The eastern Mediterranean at the time was suffering great disruption from plague and famine, and the trickle of migrants into the Delta had become a flood. From semi-autonomous, the migrant communities gradually asserted their full independence under rulers who claimed to be *Egyptian* kings, complete with the time-honoured royal titulary, but called themselves the 'Hyksos'.

The Hyksos were not a single distinct people but rather the rulers who established themselves at Avaris and then beyond, although the term has come to be applied to the Asiatics in Egypt as a whole. The term itself is Egyptian; *heka khasut* means 'ruler of [or from] the foreign lands'. It is striking that the early independent kings of culturally diverse Avaris called themselves Hyksos – defining themselves as foreigners, but using the Egyptian language to do so. Such a choice of title in fact sums up the Hyksos Fifteenth Dynasty (1650–1550 BC) of Egypt very well. The rulers laid claim to the titles and cultural trappings of the pharaohs, acculturating to the extent of presenting at least a public face that was Egyptian. But they never forgot that they were foreigners – or at any rate the Egyptians, at least those to the south, never let them forget their cultural difference.

BELOW: **Scene from the tomb of Khnumhotep II showing a bird herder with a flock of herons. Egyptians depended heavily on the fish and fowl of the Nile for their diet.**

THE WAR OF HORUS AND SETH

An important cultural difference between the migrant communities of the Delta and the Egyptians was the gods they worshipped. The Hyksos chief god was Sutekh, a composite of the Syrian deity Baal Zephom, the Hittite Teshuh and the Egyptian Seth. He was primarily a weather god, and the Hyksos were perhaps initially attracted to Seth because he was a god of thunder. They also introduced foreign deities such as Astarte and the war god Reshep. But far from the popular image of violent conflict between rival religious systems, the Hyksos rulers had nothing against Egyptian deities and encouraged the temples in the territory they ruled to maintain their traditional role as centres of learning. The Rhind Mathematical Papyrus, for example, was copied by a Lower Egyptian temple scribe in the reign of Apepi.

The notion that there was an irreconcilable religious difference between Hyksos and Egyptians stems rather from a transformation of the character of the Egyptian god Seth that occurred quite late in Egyptian history. Admittedly, Seth was always an ambivalent deity to the Egyptians. He had, after all, killed and mutilated the god-king Osiris and then fought a long war with Osiris' son Horus for rule of Egypt. Seth was eventually fought to a standstill, and the council of gods ruled that Horus (and his successors, the pharaohs) should rule the settled lands, leaving Seth the wild places and desert. Seth remained a popular god in the Delta, however, and was the local patron god of Avaris, just as Amun was the chief god of Thebes. Northern veneration of Seth remained strong through the New Kingdom, with two rulers of the Nineteenth Dynasty (1295–1186 BC) even being named Sety after this chancy deity.

And yet the mythic model of Horus (as embodied in the pharaoh) locked in war with Seth (who could be defined as any enemy of Egypt, but above all the Hyksos) was powerful. As Egyptians remembered the long war to end Hyksos rule of the Delta, portraying it as a war of good against evil, *maat* against chaos, the image of the god Seth also darkened. Since he was the god of the Hyksos, he too must be a force of evil and chaos.

EXPANSION OF HYKSOS RULE

The Hyksos began to expand their rule beyond Avaris in the late 18th century BC. Once a man had proclaimed himself king of Egypt, all of Egypt's dynastic history pushed him to attain the goal of reunification, since after all the Egyptians' understanding of proper order in the world was that Egypt *ought* to be a single country under a single ruler. Hyksos sway came to reach well upriver of Memphis, which they probably retained as a bureaucratic centre after seizing control of it, even though the Hyksos kings themselves lived at Avaris. This Fifteenth Dynasty did not consist of new migrants but rather of highly Egyptianized rulers whose families had probably lived in Egypt for several generations. All of the Hyksos rulers had northwestern Semitic names except Apepi late in the dynasty, but that is one of the few remaining signs of cultural difference. They proved to be respected and efficient rulers; probably most Egyptians of the Delta were as happy under Hyksos rule as they had been under a native dynasty. They ruled the north for about a century, from 1650 to 1550 BC.

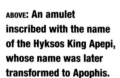

ABOVE: **An amulet inscribed with the name of the Hyksos King Apepi, whose name was later transformed to Apophis.**

RIGHT: **Scarab with the name of the Hyksos ruler Sheshi inscribed in hieroglyphs.**

One can see the power of Egypt's monarchic tradition in the nature of Hyksos rule. Despite their proclaimed foreignness, they governed very much as Egyptian pharaohs. Bureaucratic structures remained intact (although the Hyksos, while communicating in Egyptian, wrote hieroglyphs on clay tablets in the Canaanite style as well as on papyrus). They also employed the titulary of the pharaohs. Written material from the period of Hyksos rule is sparse, thanks to the conscious purge of every trace that they had ever ruled after a native dynasty was restored; the names of several Hyksos rulers are known only from scarabs. However, at least

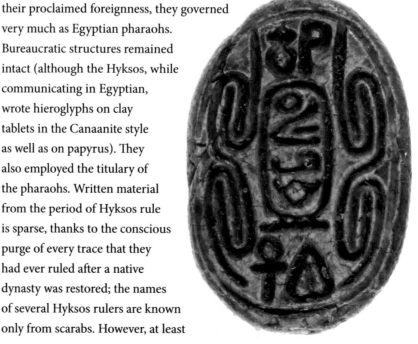

three of the six kings of the Hyksos Fifteenth Dynasty employed some of the traditional royal titulature. They had no objection, despite their veneration for Seth, to being known as 'son of Ra' and in fact performed the traditional monarchic task of restoring the temples of Egyptian deities. One scarab actually depicts a Hyksos king with the red crown of Lower Egypt and calls him 'ruler of the Delta'. Sheshi took the Horus name Mayebre, which translates as 'just is the heart of Ra'. Sekerher went even further, adopting not just a Horus name but the Two Ladies and Golden Falcon names as well.

These rulers' cultural assimilation was not just skin deep. Apepi in particular can be seen in action as a patron of Egyptian culture, encouraging a revival of the scribal tradition in Avaris. The king himself is described on a palette he presented to a scribe as the 'scribe of Ra', taught by the god Thoth himself, implying that he was fully literate in Egyptian.

The Hyksos also presented themselves as traditional pharaohs by the simple expedient of appropriating the statuary of earlier rulers, erasing the name of the first owner and adding their own. The great sphinxes originally commissioned by Amenemhat III are a striking example of this practice. Like other Middle Kingdom statuary, they found their way to Avaris, reinscribed with the name of Apepi. Such usurped pieces are the only surviving sculptures labelled clearly with the names of Hyksos kings, although it is likely that they also commissioned new statuary and it has simply not survived.

While the Hyksos proclaimed their rule over all Egypt, they were never able to make their claim good; as we will see, a rival dynasty in Upper Egypt maintained its independence and gradually became a serious threat to the Delta kings. In the reign of Khyan, probably second king of the dynasty, Hyksos forces pushed as far south as Thebes, but were unable to hold it. They were more successful with the region around Heliopolis, which they secured by means of a massive fortress they constructed nearby at the site now known as Tell el-Yahudiyya. The Canaanite-style pots found among the debris of this fort attest to an Asiatic presence. Hyksos dominion apparently reached as far as the Middle Egyptian town of Cusae, just south of Beni Hassan.

ABOVE: **Statuette of lion holding a Nubian captive, late Middle Kingdom (*c.*1850–1550 BC). The arms of this Nubian boy are held freely at his sides with the palms turned outward in a gesture of voluntary submission. The lion takes up a protective posture.**

FORGING AND DEEPENING DIPLOMATIC TIES

The Hyksos appear for the most part to have kept the loyalty of local elites, at least when those elites saw no other real alternative as pharaoh. The northern kings seem to have relied more on gifts than on fear. Their presents, such as the fine bronze dagger of Nakhman, glorify the king as well as marking the recipient out as someone who enjoyed special royal favour. Hyksos gift-giving was on a large scale, extending far beyond the territory they actually controlled. Objects with Khyan's name inscribed have been found all over Egypt. Scarabs and other items with his name also made their way to the Levant and Knossos. Part of a vase with Khyan's titles inscribed was even uncovered at Hattusas, the Hittite capital in faraway Anatolia.

Such discoveries help underscore the increased pace of contact with the eastern Mediterranean world in the era of Hyksos rule. New regions opened for Egyptian commerce, such as Cyprus, which became an important trading partner for the first time. Trade flourished, bringing prosperity that must have resigned many Egyptians of the Delta to foreign rule. The Hyksos welcomed Canaanites as well as other ethnic groups into their territory, giving them responsible positions alongside native Egyptians. The pace of diplomacy also picked up and this may have been the time at which Egypt adopted the use of Akkadian as a diplomatic lingua franca. In short, the Hyksos helped propel Egypt into a new age of deeper contacts with the Mediterranean and Near East.

The Hyksos rulers also established friendly relations with the Nubian kingdom of Kush, circumventing the native Egyptian dynasts who still ruled

BELOW: **The tomb of the noble Huy depicts Nubians presenting tribute to the king, probably either Akhenaten or Tutankhamun of the Eighteenth Dynasty. They are purposely presented as exotic, wearing animal skins and offering a giraffe along with more mundane gifts.**

Trade flourished, bringing prosperity that must have resigned many Egyptians of the Delta to foreign rule.

in Upper Egypt by sending caravans along an overland route via the western oases instead of sailing on the Nile. Already, the first Hyksos pharaoh, Sekerher, had established diplomatic links with the Kushites; his seals have been found at Kerma, the Kushite capital. Kush had become a major power, starting in Upper Nubia and increasing its wealth and standing as the main supplier of southern luxury goods to the Egyptian Middle Kingdom. During the Thirteenth Dynasty, that strong state had expanded northwards, driving out the Egyptians who had controlled Lower Nubia. Kush was probably a greater threat to the small Egyptian state of Upper Egypt than the Hyksos were. Indeed, the embattled southern Egyptian pharaohs found it necessary to fortify Edfu, only 116km (72 miles) south of Thebes, because of the threat of Nubian raids. The Kushites seem to have established their authority over a considerable swathe of Egyptian territory, from the first cataract northwards to a point not far south of Edfu. Perhaps the Nubian threat was the greater because the Kushite kings too had chosen to emulate Egyptian royal traditions, employing a number of Egyptian officials in a bureaucracy modelled on that of Egypt and even choosing to be buried in pyramids.

ABOVE: **Alabaster lid for a pyxis, inscribed with the cartouche of the Hyksos King Khyan. It was found under the foundation wall of the palace at Knossos, Crete, attesting to the wide diplomatic range of the Hyksos rulers of Lower Egypt.**

THE SIXTEENTH DYNASTY (1650–1580) IN THEBES

Nonetheless, a native dynasty endured in Upper Egypt, hemmed in to both north and south by strong foreign-ruled states that counted among their subjects probably well over half of the populace of Egypt. The members of the Sixteenth Dynasty, ruling little more than the city-state of Thebes, regarded themselves as the true heirs of the Thirteenth Dynasty. The last king of the Thirteenth Dynasty, Ay, had after all relocated his capital from Itjtawy to Thebes, doubtless driven southwards by Hyksos pressure. Little is known of these petty rulers. A list of 15 kings were later regarded as comprising the Sixteenth Dynasty. Most of them, however, are completely unknown beyond their names. And they certainly competed with other petty kings who controlled other cities of Upper Egypt.

Thebes had several important assets to offer its rulers, however. It was a substantial city with a significant agricultural population in and around it. It was the headquarters for the worship of Amun, who in the course of the Middle Kingdom had been established throughout Egypt as one of the most important deities of the pantheon. Perhaps most critically, Thebes had a tradition of ruling all Egypt, and had been the base from which Mentuhotep II had reunified the land to usher in the Middle Kingdom. Such memories and traditions would have been important, especially as Thebes was filled with monuments to the greatness of the land Mentuhotep II had united under his rule. Unfortunately, however, the Theban dynasties – the Sixteenth and the Seventeenth that succeeded it – did not have access to Memphis, the centre of scribal learning and royal archives. As a result, Thebes had to develop new rituals, especially creating distinctive royal funerary practices.

The kings of the Sixteenth Dynasty conceived of a goddess who was the personification of Thebes, Waset, who embodied strength and power. But there was little actual power to their position in the decades after they had claimed the royal titles. Though the rulers used the epithet 'beloved of his army', that army could not have amounted to a great deal in the early years. The Theban pharaohs did not have the resources for more. Especially in the first part of the Second Intermediate Period, the archaeological record reveals a remarkable dearth of objects made of precious metals in Upper Egypt as a

OPPOSITE: The Stela of Four Women, Middle Kingdom. The two women and two girls wear the long sheath dresses typical for female Egyptians. The girls have shaved heads except for a single 'lock of childhood'. They stand around a table heaped with food offerings for the dead.

OVERLEAF: An aerial view of the tombs of Roy, Shuroy and Nubkheperre Intef (with its reconstructed pyramid).

BELOW: Illustration of a group of western Asians trading in Egypt. This famous tomb painting was reproduced as a school poster in c.1930, used to teach social studies. The image is often used to depict Israel's entry into Egypt at the time of the biblical Joseph.

whole. Even allowing for the depredations of tomb robbers, the absence especially of gold is striking. Nor was there much building work during the course of the Sixteenth Dynasty; kings were not producing monumental tombs for themselves and seem to have done little by way of temple restoration or making the traditional gift of statues to temples.

SEVENTEENTH DYNASTY REVIVAL

Gradually, however, the Theban kingdom strengthened, and with the establishment of the Seventeenth Dynasty started displaying a real ambition to act as traditional pharaohs. In time, perhaps from an early stage, they revived the dream of rule over a unified Egypt. We can see the growing confidence of the Theban kings already with Rahotep, who probably founded the Seventeenth Dynasty. Rahotep boasted that he had restored the temple of Osiris at Abydos and Min's shrine at Koptos, thus fulfilling an essential pharaonic role. His successor, Sobekemsaf I, presented statues to several temples. The kings remained obscure, however; the Seventeenth Dynasty included at least nine rulers and so little is known of them that there is not even complete agreement about the order in which they reigned. Still, building activity was on the increase by the time Intef VII came to the throne, probably the fourth ruler of the dynasty. He was responsible for several small chapels and sanctuaries, and added a number of steles to the great temple complex of Amun at Karnak. Intef also provided an elaborate tomb for himself at Dra Abu el-Naga (western Thebes), which included a small mudbrick pyramid capped by a limestone pyramidion and flanked by two moderate obelisks.

By the time of Sobekemsaf II, the Theban king was able to send an admittedly rather small quarrying expedition to Wadi Hammamat.

The inner coffins were inlaid with gold and silver, and the mummy's wrappings included numerous amulets. Grave offerings included vases of gold, silver and bronze.

Sobekemsaf also had access to sufficient resources that he could arrange to be buried in some style with his queen, Nubemhat, in a small pyramid with very respectable grave goods. The objects buried with the couple have not survived – they were robbed in the time of Rameses IX – but two remarkable papyri from the Twentieth Dynasty (1186–1069 BC) report the trials of the men who looted the royal tombs. They relate that Sobekemsaf II's burial had included a gold face mask and that his mummified remains were covered with gold. The inner coffins were inlaid with gold and silver, and the mummy's wrappings included numerous amulets. Grave offerings included vases of gold, silver and bronze. The total would have amounted to about 13.6kg (30lb) of gold. Flinders Petrie uncovered the intact burial of an unnamed queen of the mid-Seventeenth Dynasty in 1909 that confirmed the impression of relative wealth. The woman's remains were in a fine gilded coffin worked in a feathered pattern, and she was laid to rest with jewellery of very high quality. Clearly, both wealth and skills were reviving in Upper Egypt.

The Seventeenth Dynasty created a new capital at Deir el-Ballas, about 48km (30 miles) north of Thebes, perhaps intending it as a forward base to launch an attack on the Hyksos. This new construction too reveals considerable wealth and an ability to tap into the labour services that pharaohs traditionally demanded of their subjects. The site, resting within an enclosing wall about 274 x 122m (900 x 400ft), was home to a double palace – the northern structure serving as royal residence and the southern as administrative centre. There was also a village for palace staff and artisans. The whole town was abandoned after reunification had been achieved, making its warlike purpose more likely. All such architectural activities point to the fact that by the latter part of the Seventeenth Dynasty the kings of the south had a fully functional state, with economic and administrative resources and logistical structures to support a significant court. These sinews of government must have developed over a number of reigns. By the mid-point of the dynasty, those royal resources also included a military force that had been at least partly reorganized and rendered much more formidable.

OPPOSITE: Sobekemsaf I, second ruler of the Seventeenth Dynasty and father of Intef VI and Intef VII. His Horus name, 'Powerful is Ra, Rescuer of the Two Lands', demonstrates the dynasty's long-term aspiration to reunite Egypt.

BELOW: Painted coffin lid of Intef VIII. The feather design on the coffin is typical of the Second Intermediate Period. He probably reigned only a few months, which might explain the simplicity of his burial.

EGYPT'S NEW MODEL ARMY

Egypt had fielded substantial armies in the Middle Kingdom, and a large administrative network dealt with recruitment and logistics for the military. The army itself, however, remained very simple. Most soldiers were conscripts, although some professional troops were introduced by the end of the Twelfth Dynasty. They were not very well equipped. Based on the remains of the soldiers buried in the vicinity of Mentuhotep II's tomb, Egyptians of the Middle Kingdom were not accustomed to fighting with body armour. Soldiers simply wore leather shirts and kilts. Their weapons too were very rudimentary: axes with copper heads, daggers and simple bows that shot arrows tipped with flint or ebony. Indeed, they did not need more elaborate equipment, since they were already at least as well equipped as the occasional Libyan or nomadic raiders they confronted and their superior numbers assured victories over the Nubians.

The military situation was far different in the Near and Middle East, however. There, petty kingdom constantly fought petty kingdom, putting a premium on the development of military technologies that would provide an advantage over an enemy otherwise of equal strength. By the time the Middle Kingdom ended, the increasingly professionalized soldiers of the Near East were wearing bronze body armour and helmets and fought with bronze swords cast with a hooked shape for greater stability, which provided them with a longer cutting surface than anything the Egyptians had. Most frightening of all, the kings of the Levant and beyond had begun to maintain elite chariot corps. Chariots – lightly built of leather woven within a bent-wood frame and pulled by two horses – could devastate infantry, especially infantry without armour. Their technique was to circle slower troops at a distance, one man driving while a second shot with a strong compound bow that had a greater range than the Egyptian simple bow. The Hyksos kings, coming from the world of such warfare, employed all these military novelties in Egypt.

It was the Seventeenth Dynasty's seminal accomplishment to adopt and adapt these Near Eastern military innovations. While horses had probably been seen in Egypt, they would have been rare, so we must imagine an extensive policy of horse-trading (and horse theft) as the Thebans learned how to use horses in war. They not only adopted the use of chariots from the Hyksos but improved their design, making them lighter, quicker, more manoeuvrable and more stable. They began to equip their troops with bronze swords, armour and helmets. And when they were ready, they began to use these tools of war for the cause of reunification.

OPPOSITE: **The Abbott Papyrus, *c.*1100 BC, tells of tomb robberies in the Twentieth Dynasty and gives evidence about a number of royal tombs of the Middle Kingdom and Second Intermediate Period.**

THEBAN RECONQUEST

For the Sixteenth and at least half of the Seventeenth Dynasty, the Theban rulers appear to have lived at relative peace with the Hyksos Fifteenth Dynasty of the north. There were certainly tensions, and at least occasionally the Hyksos rulers attempted to push into Upper Egypt. They apparently tried to suborn southern elites as well, rather than simply employing military means to expand their territory. A chance find, the Koptos Decree, reports that Teti, the administrator of Koptos in the service of the Theban pharaoh Intef VII, threw his lot in with the Hyksos. When Intef found out, he charged Teti with treason, seizing his lands and revoking his titles. The threat of such treason must have been ever present, and doubtless the Theban rulers were doing their best to win over northern nobles to their rule at the same time the Hyksos plotted with the Upper Egyptians.

When the reconquest began, it took at least 30 years and involved three successive pharaohs – Taa, Kamose and Ahmose. A tale written much later in the Nineteenth Dynasty gives a puzzling explanation for why war broke out. The text, known as 'The Quarrel of Apepi and Seqenenra' (Seqenenra was the Horus name of Taa), relates that the Hyksos king Apepi sent an insulting letter to the Theban king. Apepi could not sleep, he said, because of the roaring of the hippopotami in Thebes (which was 644km/ 400 miles away from Avaris). It is not clear today why this was regarded as so insulting; perhaps a demand that the hippos be silenced should be interpreted as a brash claim of overlordship, assuming that Taa would do the bidding of the Hyksos, no matter how arrogant and unreasonable that demand might be. It is quite possible that the Theban kings

BELOW: **Wooden coffin of Intef VII, now on display in the British Museum. Traces of the original gilding still survive, suggesting that the Theban pharaohs of the Seventeenth Dynasty tried to present themselves as wealthy, but did so on a budget.**

The death of a king on the battlefield was a horrid, cataclysmic affront to *maat*, so shocking that it was not recorded in writing.

ABOVE: **The mummified remains of Seqenenra Taa at the Egyptian Museum in Cairo. The axe and spear blows that killed the pharaoh are still clearly visible on his mummy.**

were in fact vassals who paid tribute to the Hyksos, and Apepi was rather crassly asserting his rights. Whatever the case, Taa was ready for war.

It is hoped that Taa enjoyed some initial success, but if he did it did not last very long. He was still only between 30 and 40 years old when – shockingly for a pharaoh – Taa was killed in battle. The death of a king on the battlefield was a horrid, cataclysmic affront to *maat*, so shocking that it was not recorded in writing. Taa's own body tells the tale of his last moments of life, however. His mummified remains were discovered in the royal cache at Deir el-Bahri in 1881, where priests had hidden the bodies of a number of kings and queens, several hundred years after Taa's death, to protect them from tomb robbers. Identified by the inscription on his coffin, it was immediately obvious that Taa's end in *c.*1560 BC had been violent. The body bore five major wounds, showing that the pharaoh had been struck down with axes, spears and maybe a mace. Of the two axe cuts, one fractured his skull, whereupon he would have fallen to the ground. The other four wounds were delivered horizontally, when he was already lying on his right side. He was attacked viciously; other

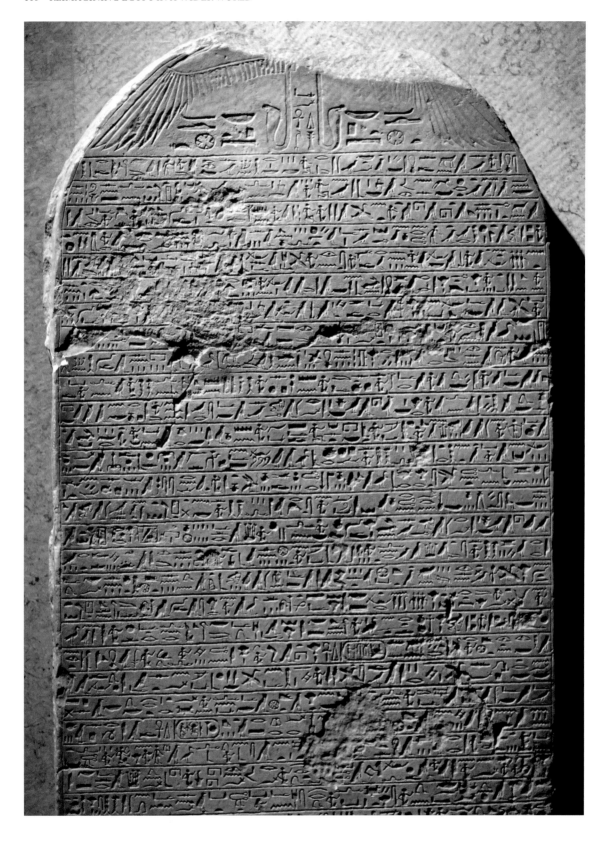

blows damaged the bridge of his nose, his left cheek, the right side of his head and his ribs and vertebrae. After his death, the body had then lain several days before being collected for burial; decomposition had already begun before the embalmers began their work.

The cause had suffered a serious setback, but reunification was the dream of the whole dynasty rather than of a single individual. The south's belligerence was certainly enough to make the Hyksos begin to worry, as can be seen from their decision, late in the period they ruled the Delta, to construct a massive citadel at the western edge of previously unfortified Avaris. The whole site covered over 48,562 sq m (12 acres), and its thick walls and bastions made a formidable obstacle. They also sought a military alliance with Kush; a stele erected in the reign of Kamose tells how a courier was intercepted with the message that Hyksos and Kushite should unite, since Thebes was attacking the former without provocation. Kush and the Delta could then divide up Egypt between them after Kamose had been defeated. And indeed, Taa's successor Kamose soon renewed the struggle. We do not actually know who Kamose was. Usually it is assumed that he was Taa's son, but if so his mother was not Taa's sister-wife Ahhotep. Instead, as we will see, the timing of events suggests that it was Kamose's own successor Ahmose who was Taa's son, and Kamose was perhaps Taa's brother, called to the throne because his nephew was too young to rule and the military situation demanded a male ruler rather than a female regent.

Kamose's rule was short, a mere three years, but it was highly active. At the start of his reign, the new pharaoh campaigned to the south, heightening the impression that the Kushites were a greater threat than the Hyksos. By the third year of his reign he had pushed the Kushites back and recaptured the great fortress of Buhen at the second cataract. Once again Egypt began to receive shipments of Nubian gold, providing vital funds for the army, and Kamose was able to integrate units of Nubian light infantry, the Medjay, into his own forces. The engagement with the Nubians appears to have lulled the Hyksos into a false sense of security, because Kamose had no intention of leaving them in peace. As he proclaims on the stele he had erected at Karnak: 'How can I claim to be powerful, when there is a ruler in Avaris and another in Kush?' In grandiose terms, he announced that the time had come to liberate Egypt, crush the Asiatics and rip open the belly of the Hyksos king Apepi.

Overriding his advisers' urging to make a treaty with the Delta king, Kamose instead launched a great surprise raid that took the Hyksos completely off guard. According to Kamose's victory stele, the raid penetrated Hyksos territory as far as Avaris itself, approaching the city closely enough to see the palace women looking down from the windows. The raid garnered a

OPPOSITE: **Kamose erected this stela at Karnak to celebrate his victories over the Hyksos ruler Apepi, boasting that he had raided as far as Avaris itself.**

THE WOMEN OF THE RECONQUEST

Two extraordinary women, Tetisheri and her daughter Ahhotep, played a vital role in Thebes' war against the Hyksos, for which they received public recognition and praise that makes them more visible than most of Egypt's royal women. Tetisheri, often called 'Mother of the New Kingdom', was the wife of Senakhtenre and mother of Taa as well as Ahhotep. She was a commoner, the daughter of a judge named Tjenna and his wife Neferu. It is not clear what role she performed, but when she died at the age of 70, her grandson Ahmose issued decrees telling of her great service to Egypt. She was supplied with a lavish tomb at Thebes and a cenotaph at Abydos – a pyramid, no less, with a full staff of priests for her mortuary establishment. One can speculate that Tetisheri, as queen grandmother, had played an important role holding the Theban state together in the unsettled years between the death of Kamose and Ahmose coming of age.

We are on firmer ground with Ahhotep, full sister and senior wife of Taa. She served as regent for her son Ahmose, probably for as long as ten years. During her regency, she kept the peace with the Hyksos, but when Ahmose resumed the campaign she recruited for the army and kept order in Upper Egypt. On the great stele he had erected at Karnak, her son Ahmose praised Ahhotep as 'the one who performed the rites and cared for Egypt'. The inscription even says that Ahhotep was responsible for pacifying Upper Egypt and expelling rebels, which makes it likely that she actually commanded troops in battle. Further evidence of the queen mother's military role comes from her tomb at Thebes, discovered in 1859, which had been constructed as part of an extensive mortuary complex. Within her coffin, the excavators found a gold battle-axe and three pieces of 'gold of valour', the special ornaments given to soldiers for outstanding bravery. It is hard to escape the conclusion that these royal women were propelled into a public role by the desperate struggle against the Hyksos, and that they more than lived up to expectations.

OPPOSITE: Limestone statuette of Queen Tetisheri, who played an important role in the decades of campaigning to reunify Egypt.

LEFT: This golden axe was found in the tomb of Queen Ahhotep, mother of Ahmose, at Dra Abu el-Naga. Along with the gold of valour also found with the queen's remains, the axe provides a strong suggestion that the queen mother commanded troops in the field.

great deal of loot and the southern pharaoh burned the Hyksos ships in their harbour. One must always beware of taking official Egyptian boasting too literally, however, and some scholars believe that Kamose's raid got no further than Cynopolis in Middle Egypt, far from Avaris itself.

It is likely that Kamose was killed in battle, like his predecessor, before the reconquest could advance much further. His mummified remains were found in the second royal cache at Dra Abu el-Naga. However, Kamose's body had been embalmed so badly that it disintegrated when it was removed from its coffin. In other words, he very likely died in the field, far from the professional Theban morticians.

THE DEFEAT OF THE HYKSOS

After Kamose's death, there was a pause in warfare, probably because Ahmose was still too young to take an active military or governmental role. It was only in the 11th year of his reign that the Theban pharaoh took to war again. An entry on the back of the Rhind Mathematical Papyrus, which was written in Hyksos territory, tells how 'he of the South' took first Heliopolis and then Sile. Presumably other Hyksos towns resisted, because it was not until sometime between Ahmose's 18th and 22nd regnal year that the army of Upper Egypt was ready to attack Avaris itself. What happened then is unclear, but the last Hyksos king, Khamudi, appears to have negotiated an agreement that allowed him and his followers to leave the city in safety.

Excavation of the site bears out that picture of surrender rather than violent assault, as archaeologists have found no evidence of large-scale destruction. However, Ahmose did order the demolition of the city's fortification and citadel. When Ahmose had a new palace constructed for himself over the ruins of the Hyksos citadel, though, excavators found an ominous hint that all might not have been peaceful – a number of human hands had been purposely buried on the site as a foundation deposit. We also have the testimony of one of Ahmose's commanders, Ahmose son of Ibana, whose detailed tomb autobiography is our best source for the reconquest. The commander was present at the taking of Avaris and boasts that he seized four people as slaves there, one man and three women. Most likely, the important officials, courtiers, nobles and their families and soldiers were allowed to depart from the city in peace, leaving the commoners as spoils for the triumphant Egyptians. Soon after the city's capture, evidence of a mixed Egyptian and Asiatic populace in Avaris ends.

The war was not quite over. After the Hyksos quitted Avaris, they retreated to Sharuhen, an important fortified town in southwestern Palestine. Perhaps fearing that the Hyksos king would use Sharuhen as a base for reconquest

OPPOSITE: **'The Expulsion of the Hyksos' by Patrick Gray, 1906.**

OVERLEAF: **Painted engravings in the tomb of Ahmose, son of Ebana, in the El Kab necropolis on the east bank of the Nile at Aswan.**

The Egyptians chased the Hyksos further into Syria, and the 'kings of foreign lands' vanished from history.

of the Delta, Ahmose and his army pursued the enemy there, besieging the city for three years. After it fell, the Egyptians chased the Hyksos further into Syria, and the 'kings of foreign lands' vanished from history. Ahmose then re-established the Middle Kingdom's fortresses on Egypt's northeastern border, a defence against any future invasion. The final defeat of the Hyksos also gave Ahmose a claim to their territories in Canaan. Thus Egypt had a permanent foothold in western Asia for the first time in its recorded history.

Not all Egyptians were sorry to see their Hyksos lords go. Ahmose actually had to suspend the siege of Avaris so he could go and suppress a rebellion in the Egyptian town of Elkab. Ahmose's stele honouring the queen mother Ahhotep also suggests further rebel activity in Upper Egypt during the reconquest period. And after the conquest was complete, Ahmose still had to deal with two rebellions. One, led by a foreigner named Aata, was a minor affair. The second, however, instigated by an Egyptian named Teti-an, was serious. Ahmose's inscription tells that Teti-an gathered malcontents under his banner; perhaps they were men who had served the Hyksos king, who had lost privilege and perhaps property and livelihood at the hands of the king who now ruled a united Egypt once more. The rebellion failed, but Ahmose did not live long to enjoy his success. He was only about 35 years old when he died. His remains show that the great unifier suffered from both arthritis and scoliosis, making his military accomplishments even more impressive.

NEW RULE IN THE NEW KINGDOM

For the rulers of the New Kingdom, which had its official start with Ahmose's reunification, the Second Intermediate Period was an age of national trauma. The pharaohs became much less tolerant of foreigners in their midst; it is theorized that the Hebrews had settled in Egypt under Hyksos auspices, only to suffer prejudice and semi-slavery as the new Eighteenth Dynasty (1550– 1295 BC) turned against the Asiatics in their midst. The need to prevent a recurrence of the Hyksos disruption of *maat* served as justification for the new rulers' aggressive foreign policy, and more than 80 years later, Hatshepsut in her inscriptions condemned the Hyksos as people who 'ruled without Ra' and boasted of their expulsion. The distorted memory of this first period of foreign rule cast a much longer shadow on subsequent ages than their actual rule had, ushering in the way for the glories of the New Kingdom.

LEFT: This slightly larger than life-size head of Pharaoh Ahmose I was apparently influenced by the statuary of Mentuhotep II, Ahmose's predecessor as unifier of Egypt. The figure wears the white crown of Upper Egypt.

THE AGE OF EGYPTIAN EMPIRE

Ahmose's victory over the Hyksos ushered in the period known as the New Kingdom (1550–1069 BC). Nor was the expulsion of the northern Hyksos rulers the only accomplishment of Ahmose's short life; he took decisive steps that allowed his Eighteenth Dynasty (1550–1295 BC) to flourish. This great pharaoh's reorganization of Egyptian government punished nomarchs who had served the Hyksos, firmly reasserting royal power over the whole kingdom and ruling instead through judges and governors sworn to royal service. Even more important for Egypt's future, Ahmose took steps to assure Egypt's safety from both the kingdom of Kush to the south and the states of west Asia. Ahmose restored the Egyptian fortresses in Nubia and established the position of viceroy of Kush.

OPPOSITE: **A masterpiece of New Kingdom art, this funeral mask covered the head of Pharaoh Tutankhamun. Crafted from two layers of highly refined gold and ornamented with lapis lazuli, carnelian, turquoise, obsidian and glass paste, the mask weighs over 10kg (22lb).**

RIGHT: **Sphinx of Hatshepsut, New Kingdom, c.1479–1458 BC. This colossal sphinx portrays the female pharaoh Hatshepsut with the body of a lion and a human head wearing a *nemes* headcloth and false beard.**

The foundation Ahmose laid enabled the true conquest of Nubia, the major campaigns in the reigns of Thutmose I, II, III and Hatshepsut leading to a period of 400 years during which Egypt finally actually ruled Nubia. To the north, Ahmose razed the Hyksos citadel at Avaris, but established a major military base there, a bastion to guard against Asian invasion that under his successors became a staging ground for military expeditions far into Asia. As a result, at the height of the New Kingdom, Egypt's pharaohs ruled an area of about 640,000 sq km (400,000 sq miles), stretching from Khartoum (in modern Sudan) to Carchemish on the Euphrates, and westwards as far as the Siwa Oasis. Those victories did not come easily, as Egypt's enemies were now equal or even superior to Egypt in military might. Thus, it was an age of warrior pharaohs, but also of negotiators who could no longer simply dictate terms to weaker foes.

ABOVE: Fragment of a relief depicting King Ahmose wearing the crown of Lower Egypt, from his cenotaph at Abydos. Although New Kingdom pharaohs were buried at Thebes, they continued to erect funerary monuments at Abydos, around the supposed tomb of Osiris.

THE REIGN OF AMENHOTEP I

Ahmose died when he was only about 35 years old, and it is likely that his sister-queen Ahmose-Nefertari served as regent in the first years of their son Amenhotep I's reign (1525–1504 BC). Ahmose-Nefertari had been very active in the task of rebuilding Egypt after the reconquest. She was the first royal woman to hold the title 'God's Wife of Amun', a powerful office that gave its incumbent not just religious prestige, but also at least a degree of control over the enormous holdings of the priesthood of Egypt's chief deity. The queen-mother lived for most of her son's reign, and was acknowledged as the 'female chieftain of Upper and Lower Egypt'. Perhaps most tellingly, after the death of Amenhotep I, he and his mother were both deified and worshipped at Thebes as the patron deities of the tomb-workers' village at Deir el-Medina. In life, Ahmose-Nefertari appears to have had at least some share of human vanity; her mummified remains show that, by the time of her death at about the age of 65, she was almost bald, but wore a wig made of human hair.

Amenhotep I's reign saw significant military advances, and, like his father, the pharaoh led armies personally. In the first year of his reign, Egypt was invaded by a confederation of Libyan tribes, perhaps probing for weaknesses at the end of Ahmose's strong rule. Soon, the Kingdom of Kush also tried to make a resurgence, expanding into the area south of Aswan. They were halted, however, and the trade routes to the south were secured. Amenhotep's successes in Nubia led to an improvement in the Egyptian

LEFT: **Emphasizing the divinity of pharaohs, this lintel from the temple complex at Karnak depicts the deified Amenhotep I actually wearing the headdress of the great god Amun-Ra. It was erected by Amenhotep's son Senusret I.**

economy, as gold and other Nubian products began to flow more freely to the north. Thanks to this new prosperity, Amenhotep I was able to build extensively at Karnak and elsewhere.

THE MILITARY MIGHT OF THUTMOSE I (1504–1492 BC)

Amenhotep I did not have a son to succeed him, so instead he designated a successor, a proven military leader. The new pharaoh, Thutmose I, married the princess Ahmose, who was probably either Amenhotep I's daughter or sister. There appears to have been a peaceful transition of power and, despite the break in bloodline, Thutmose's and successive reigns are regarded as still part of the Eighteenth Dynasty. Thutmose's choice as king was a good one, as he proved to be a success both administratively and militarily. To the south, Thutmose I continued the onslaught against the Kingdom of Kush, conquering and devastating the Kushite capital at Kerma. The Kushite king was captured and executed, and his body slung by the feet from the prow of Thutmose's flagship, a demonstration that the Kushites were regarded as rebels rather than as legitimate foreign enemies. Thutmose's troops penetrated upstream as far as Kurgus between the fourth and fifth cataracts, and he must have felt justified in regarding the reconquest of Nubia as complete, although within two years he had to return with his army; Nubia never resigned itself to Egyptian rule.

Thutmose's greatest campaigns were waged in west Asia, however, and he even moved the court from Thebes to the more northerly Memphis, probably to be closer to the northern enemy. Once more leading his troops personally, Thutmose fought several times in Syria and Palestine; he was probably responsible for the evidence of destruction at 20 or so Palestinian sites from the period. He did not, however, establish permanent garrisons; his goal appears rather to have been to avenge the shame of Hyksos domination of Egyptian, and doubtless to prevent the formation of a major state in west Asia that could challenge Egypt. Thutmose's troops marched as far as the Euphrates, and were astonished to see that the river ran from north to south – clearly the wrong direction for people who had only ever known the Nile.

FEMALE RULE UNDER HATSHEPSUT

Following Thutmose I was one of the few – and certainly the best-attested – female rulers of Egyptian history, Hatshepsut. Hatshepsut did not immediately succeed on her father's death. Her brother, the son of Thutmose I and Queen Ahmose, died before his father, and the next pharaoh, Thutmose II (1492–1479 BC), was a son by a minor wife. The princess Hatshepsut was married to this half-brother, as was the custom in the Eighteenth Dynasty. After only a little more than a decade on the throne, however, Thutmose II died, at which point the control of Egypt became interesting. The late pharaoh *did* leave a son to inherit the throne, Thutmose III (1479–1425 BC), the child of a lesser wife. Hatshepsut, the king's great wife as well as birth member of the royal family, claimed the regency for the new boy pharaoh. From the start, however, she firmly asserted her importance, taking precedence over the young king and adopting the title 'Mistress of the Two Lands', a striking parallel to the pharaoh's own title. She even commissioned two obelisks for the entrance to the temple of Amun, an unprecedented move for somebody who was not

ruler but only regent. Then, by the end of Thutmose III's seventh regnal year, Hatshepsut claimed the throne for herself, displacing her still-young stepson and ruling in her own name from 1473 to 1458 BC.

We do not know what forces pushed Hatshepsut to take this step; perhaps a military crisis demanded stronger leadership than a regent could provide. As reigning queen, she certainly did not play the 'evil stepmother'. Although she erected monuments in her own name, she gave Thutmose III increasingly responsible tasks, including command of the army – which strongly suggests that they had a friendly relationship and that she did not fear overthrow at his hands. But Hatshepsut, a short, rather plump woman, held the reins of Egypt firmly for 22 years. Soon, her inscriptions proclaimed that her father Thutmose I had in fact proclaimed Hatshepsut his heir before he died. Even more strikingly, in the art that decorated Hatshepsut's magnificent mortuary

ABOVE: **Painting of Queen Hatshepsut, here depicted as a male pharaoh, making an offering to the god Horus, from the queen's mortuary temple at Deir el-Bahri.**

OVERLEAF: **The mortuary temple of Queen Hatshepsut at Deir el-Bahri. Designed by the royal steward Senenmut, the temple was built into the cliff face; it stands 30m (97ft) tall and is approached by long terraces that were originally lined with gardens.**

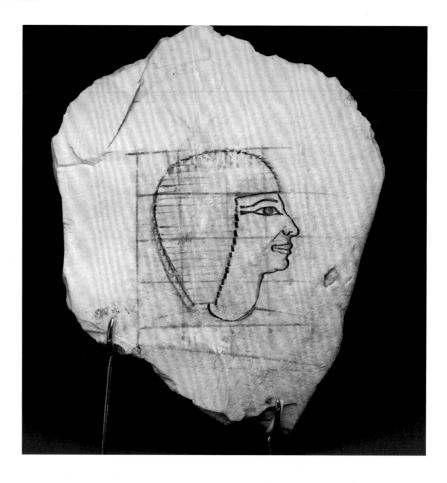

ABOVE: **Egyptian artists followed rigorous rules for proportion, which varied little over the millennia. We can see how an artist approached the task in this gridded sketch of Senenmut, Hatshepsut's steward.**

chapel at Deir el-Bahri, we are informed that the god Amun himself fathered Hatshepsut (taking the form of a shower of gold) on Queen Ahmose, the great wife of Thutmose I. And, since pharaohs were by definition masculine, the reliefs depicting Hatshepsut's childhood show her as a boy. In her statuary, at first the queen was shown as a female with male clothing and regalia, but soon came to be depicted with the body of a male pharaoh, although retaining the feminine form of her names and titles.

Hatshepsut enjoyed a mostly peaceful and prosperous reign. She inherited a number of her father's high officials, some of whom continued in Thutmose III's employ after she died. As is too often the case with female rulers, however, speculation developed then and now that her chief adviser, Senenmut, had become rather more than a servant. Senenmut certainly amassed a great deal of power, holding more than 80 titles. He eventually fell from grace, however, perhaps after he committed the transgression of trying to link his own tomb with that of his queen. As so often in the history of Egypt, we are left with a mystery: Senenmut never occupied the tomb he had prepared; instead, a mummified horse was found there.

Since Egypt was mostly at peace during her reign, Hatshepsut could exploit Egypt's resources for large-scale building projects. She bragged that she was responsible for restoring the temples of Middle Egypt that had been devastated by the Hyksos more than 80 years before – although, as we have seen, the amount of Hyksos destruction is questionable. Most notably, Hatshepsut's mortuary temple, which she named *djeser djeseru* ('holy of holies'), is still largely intact at Deir el-Bahri. On the walls of the Deir el-Bahri temple, besides proclaiming her right to the throne, Hatshepsut boasted of the accomplishments of her reign. One of the most striking scenes depicts a large trading expedition Hatshepsut sent south to distant Punt, which returned with myrrh and myrrh-trees, ivory, ebony, rare minerals and exotic animals. The queen's government also exploited the turquoise mines of Sinai and waged perhaps as many as four campaigns in Nubia, at least one of which was led by Hatshepsut in person.

Some modern Egyptologists believe that Hatshepsut groomed her daughter Nefrura to succeed her, which might carry modern notions of female empowerment too far. The princess was certainly named as God's Wife of Amun, but was probably intended as a mate for Thutmose III rather than further displacing him. However, Nefrura died in Hatshepsut's 16th regnal year, leaving Thutmose as the only viable successor.

Hatshepsut died, probably of natural causes, when she was in her mid-50s, and Thutmose III at last took the throne. It used to be thought that Thutmose lashed out against the memory of his stepmother, showing his resentment

BELOW: Romans of the imperial age were fascinated by obelisks and transported a number of them to the city of Rome, including this obelisk of Thutmose III. It was originally placed in the Circus Maximus, but now stands before the archbasilica of St John Lateran.

THE VALLEY OF THE KINGS

The pharaohs of the New Kingdom still indulged in extremely costly and luxurious burials, but had learned that their status as god-kings did not protect their remains from tomb robbers. So, they displayed their greatness with splendid mortuary temples, but prepared a place for their actual remains in carefully hidden rock-cut tombs on the west bank of the Nile opposite Thebes, in an area known today as the Valley of the Kings. To date, the tombs of 63 royal personages and particularly privileged nobles have been uncovered in the Valley; most royal wives were interred in the nearby Valley of the Queens. The tombs range in size from simple pits to elaborate subterranean edifices such as KV5, the tomb designed for the many sons of Rameses II. Almost all the tombs were pillaged in antiquity; to date, the only intact tomb found there is that of Tutankhamun.

The Valley of the Kings was used for primary burials for about 500 years, perhaps starting in the reign of Amenhotep I; in later periods, the remains of many lesser individuals were intruded into the then-derelict tombs.

In the Twenty-first Dynasty (1069–945 BC), the priests of Amun opened most of the tombs, moving the mummified remains to safety (and confiscating most of the wealth they discovered). The majority of the mummies found a penultimate resting place in a great 'royal cache' in the cliff overlooking Hatshepsut's temple at Deir el-Bahri. They were piled there in great disorder, with many bodies placed into the wrong coffins; over a dozen more mummies were found in the tomb of Amenhotep II. Some of the bodies have still not been identified, but evidence ranging from coffin inscriptions to scarabs to forensic analysis of the remains has allowed scholars to identify a number of the greatest rulers of the New Kingdom and to provide us with astonishing details about their age, health and other physical characteristics.

LEFT: Aerial view of the Ramesseum and Deir el-Bahari, on the west bank of the Nile across from modern Luxor.

of her usurpation by immediately defacing and destroying her monuments. Further study, however, has shown that the destruction of the queen's statues (many of which were found buried beside the Deir el-Bahri temple) and erasure of her name was not in fact a *damnatio memoriae* but instead highly selective, only removing the parts of Hatshepsut's name and titles that showed she had been king. And the destruction did not happen at all for more than 30 years after her death, making it impossible to sustain the notion that Thutmose had hated the woman who took his place. Still, Hatshepsut was left off the king lists inscribed by later pharaohs; the notion of a woman on the throne was clearly perceived as an affront to the right order of the world (*maat*).

EXPANSION UNDER THUTMOSE III (*C.*1400–1390 BC)

Thutmose III, despite the belated start to his reign, proved to be highly successful, ushering in the golden age of Egyptian empire. After his sole rule began, Thutmose led no fewer than 17 military expeditions into west Asia. In his very first year on the throne, perhaps 1479 BC (opinions on the chronology differ), he won a notable victory in the Battle of Megiddo, the first battle in history for which we have a detailed description. Thutmose was clearly concerned about accurate reporting, and had a scribe keep a daily journal; towards the end of his reign, the accounts of that and other campaigns were inscribed on the inner walls of the temple of Amun at Karnak, and are now known as his *Annals*. At least 11 tombs uncovered at Thebes also tell of participation in Thutmose's conquest of Syria, adding valuable details. The tributary small kingdoms of Canaan attempted to shift their allegiance to the Hittites to their north, and Egypt was determined to keep control of the region. So, Thutmose marched north to battle a Canaanite coalition led by the prince of Kadesh. A dangerous three-day march through narrow passes allowed the pharaoh to launch a surprise frontal attack. The Egyptian victory would have been complete had the Egyptian soldiers not stopped to plunder the enemy camp, allowing the king of Kadesh and many of his men to escape to the walled city of Kadesh, which fell only after a seven-month siege. It was a victory nonetheless, and Thutmose boasted that the loot included 894 chariots, 200 suits of armour, more than 2,000 horses and over 25,000 other animals.

Thutmose's other campaigns were clearly just as successful; the king bragged that he donated more than 12.7 tonnes (14 tons) of gold to Amun's temple at Karnak in the course of his reign; even if exaggerated, the gains from war in addition to the usual revenues of the pharaohs must have been impressive. Every summer for 18 years, the campaigns in Syria continued,

OVERLEAF: Thutmose III slaughtering Canaanite captives. Although a common motif in pharaonic art, this relief commemorates a specific historic event – Thutmose's victory in the Battle of Megiddo.

Thutmose III boasted that the loot included 894 chariots, 200 suits of armour, more than 2,000 horses and over 25,000 other animals.

RIGHT: **The wars of the New Kingdom were a popular theme in history books at the turn of the last century. This scene depicts Thutmose III in battle, from Hutchinson's** *History of the Nations* **(1915).**

the army supported by an extensive naval deployment. In all, Thutmose's troops captured 350 cities (some admittedly very small), and by the end of Thutmose's campaigns the Egyptian empire had reached its largest extent. The Egyptologist James Henry Breasted dubbed Thutmose III the 'Napoleon of Egypt', thanks not just to his conquests, but also to his supposedly diminutive height. When the king's mummy was first measured, he was reported to have been only a bit over 1.52m (5ft) tall. The person doing the measuring, however, had failed to notice that the mummy's feet were missing; in reality the king was of average height, about 1.7m (5ft 7in). The chance of archaeological discovery allows us interesting glimpses of the administrators

By the end of Thutmose's campaigns the Egyptian empire had reached its largest extent.

who served Thutmose III. We can see that service to the throne often ran in families; for example, Thutmose's vizier Rekhmire was the kinsman of a man who had served Hatshepsut in the same capacity; Rekhmire's tomb at Thebes includes details of his and his family's government service. The high officials who served well were rewarded not just with wealth but also with honours, such as Benimeryt, architect and overseer of Thutmose's treasury, who was named as tutor to one of the princesses. The court was also a very cosmopolitan place. Not only did Thutmose bring young foreign nobles to be educated at his court; he also favoured men of talent even if they were not of pure Egyptian blood. Maiherpri, a man so important he merited a burial in the Valley of the Kings, had distinctive sub-Saharan African features. Later in the Eighteenth Dynasty, a pharaoh even employed a vizier with the distinctly Near Eastern name Aper-el.

BELOW: Tomb KV35 in the Valley of the Kings, discovered in 1898, was intended as the eternal resting place of Amenhotep II. The tomb had been looted, but Amenhotep's mummified remains were found in his sarcophagus. The tomb was later used as a cache for a number of other royal mummies, which were reburied to protect them from tomb robbers.

FURTHER MILITARY ADVANCES

The militarism of the New Kingdom continued into the next reign. Amenhotep II (1427–1400 BC) as prince was placed in command at the great naval base at Peru-Nefer near Memphis, a post his father had also held. He also commanded an expedition to Asia for his father to suppress a revolt. He came home proudly displaying the bodies of seven defeated petty kings hung head-down from the prow of the royal ship; he had six suspended from the temple wall at Thebes, and sent the final body on to Napata to discourage the Nubians from thoughts of rebellion.

As pharaoh, two other campaigns into Asia were also successful. The second of these was especially ambitious, intended to put down a large-scale revolt. The Egyptian army marched nearly to Aleppo, pillaging and devastating as it went. An inscription reports that Amenhotep returned home with numerous captives, 300 chariots, 745kg (1,643lb) of gold and an impressive 54,809kg (120,833lb) of silver, the last especially valuable since silver was rare in Egypt.

BELOW: **'Amenhotep III and Tiy' by Winifred Brunton. Brunton served as staff artist for her husband, the archaeologist Guy Brunton, but is best known for her recreations of Egyptian figures published in two volumes, in 1926 and 1929.**

A TIME OF PEACE AND PROSPERITY

The following two reigns were prosperous and for the most part peaceful, Thutmose IV (1400–1390 BC) and Amenhotep III (1390–1352 BC) willing to enjoy the fruits of Thutmose III's conquests. Indeed, we know relatively little of Thutmose IV's decade-long reign. He was, according to his own testimony, not the heir apparent to the throne, but divine intervention assured his ascension. As a prince, he went hunting one day, and rested beside the Great Sphinx. While there, he heard the statue complain about the condition it was in, and the stone creature then promised that Thutmose would be pharaoh if he restored it. So, the young man had the sand cleared from the figure and repaired it, placing a stela between its paws to commemorate the dream and the pious work he had undertaken.

Amenhotep III was probably only 12 years old when he inherited the throne, although there is no evidence that his mother Mutemwiya ever served as regent. It is difficult to assess Amenhotep's role as pharaoh, in large part because his reign was later overshadowed by that of his notorious son. Amenhotep seems to have been uninterested in war; his only military engagement was to put down a Nubian uprising in the fifth year of his long reign. The pharaoh maintained at least six Egyptian garrison towns in western Asia (four on the coast and two inland), but it is possible that some of the Syrian and Palestinian vassal states started breaking away from Egyptian control under Amenhotep III's indifferent gaze. The loss of Palestinian vassals was significant in the long term because they served as a vital buffer between Egypt and the growing power of the Hittites. Still, the pharaoh was able to demand tribute and 'gifts' from the petty kings of Levant, as when Amenhotep ordered the king of Gezer to send him 40 beautiful female cup-bearers besides his annual tribute.

Whether from illness or laziness, Amenhotep III left much of the government in the hands of his chief wife, Tiye. The daughter of a commoner priest, this dynamic woman appears to have been the de facto ruler, especially after Amenhotep retired to the great pleasure palace that he had constructed at Malkata. Malkata had everything a leisure-loving pharaoh could desire, a miniature city of palaces, fine homes for court officials, and even a mile-long artificial lake Amenhotep had dug to please Tiye. Tiye's name, very unusually, appears on official acts, and she corresponded with King Tushratta of Mitanni, the most important of Egypt's vassal states in west Asia. The pharaoh also gave extraordinary prominence to his closest courtier, Amenhotep son

ABOVE: **Head of Queen Tiye,
found at Medinet el Ghurob.**

Malkata had everything a leisure-loving pharaoh could desire, a miniature city of palaces, fine homes for court officials and even a mile-long artificial lake.

of Hapu, who oversaw many of the king's enormous building projects. The king gave this man the unique privilege of a personal mortuary temple, overlooking that of Amenhotep III himself, suggesting what a key role the son of Hapu played in the royal administration.

Amenhotep III identified to an extraordinary extent with the god Amun. Amun, originally a local god of Thebes, had risen steadily in importance since the Old Kingdom, thanks above all to the importance of Thebes for the pharaohs of both the Middle and the New Kingdom. In the New Kingdom, Amun acquired the attributes of many other gods, and his association with the sun god Ra led to acknowledgement that Amun-Ra was king of the gods. Amenhotep III founded a new shrine of Amun at Thebes, intended especially for celebration of the annual *opet* festival, during which the pharaoh would commune with the god and renew his own divine essence. Amenhotep appears to have taken this very literally. He was the first pharaoh to present himself as divine in his own lifetime. Art depicts him making offerings to his

BELOW: Little remains of the mortuary temple of Amenhotep III besides these two gigantic statues, the so-called Colossi of Memnon. Constructed of blocks of quartzite sandstone, each statue stands 18m (60ft) tall.

own image, and, not content with the title 'son of Ra', he called himself 'the radiant solar disc'. It is hard to avoid the thought that this short, unhealthy man – he was barely 1.52m (5ft) tall and overweight, with rotten teeth and a congenital overbite – was desperately trying to deny his mortality. Such an interpretation is supported by Amenhotep's repeated *sed* festivals, celebrated in years 30, 34 and 37 of his reign, which were also intended to restore the ageing king's link to his divine nature. Late in life, the pharaoh suffered serious illness, and had hundreds of statues of the goddess Sekhmet carved to fight the sickness demons; the king of Mitanni even sent Amenhotep two statues of Ishtar for the same purpose. To most of his subjects and to posterity, however, Amenhotep presented himself as magnificent and divine. His mortuary temple, the largest ever, covered about 0.37 sq km (91 acres). It is little but rubble now, but was a marvel for centuries. The pharaoh also commissioned more than a thousand statues of himself, many of them colossal, including the so-called Colossi of Memnon, which were placed at the entrance to the mortuary temple.

THE 'HERETIC' PHARAOH AND QUEEN NEFERTITI
One of the most fascinating figures in Egyptian history is the 'heretic' pharaoh, Amenhotep IV, who is better known by the name he took to honour his god, Akhenaten (1352–1336 BC). The new pharaoh's reign began conventionally, perhaps with a period of co-rule with his ailing father. But in his third regnal year, Akhenaten took the unprecedented step of celebrating a *sed* festival (which normally marked 30 years on the throne), probably as a public platform to initiate sweeping religious reforms. At the festival, many of the great gods of Egypt, including Amun, were excluded, in favour of Aten, the disc of the sun. By the end of his fifth year, Akhenaten (whose new name means 'glory of the sun-disc') had abolished most of the pantheon and closed temples throughout Egypt. He even launched a campaign to remove the gods' names and images from Egypt's many holy places, a task on such a grand scale that he must have employed the army. While recognizing the existence of other deities, the pharaoh insisted that Aten alone was to be worshipped – and that such worship could only be performed with pharaoh as sole mediator to the divine. Why he introduced such a radical change has been a matter for speculation for centuries, with theories ranging from personal revelation to insanity to a cold-blooded determination to end the great wealth and power of the traditional priesthoods.

Akhenaten's new religion probably had little impact on most lower-class Egyptians, except those pressed into service to build the new, pure city of Akhetaten. Excavation of the workers' village there has uncovered large

ROYAL CITIES

Because ancient Egyptian towns and cities were largely constructed of mudbrick, little trace of them remains, leading earlier Egyptologists to believe that the kingdom was mostly non-urban. Egypt was, however, full of towns, some of which grew organically, but some of which were brought into being at a pharaoh's command. The two most notable of these planned royal cities, Akhetaten and Piramesse, demonstrate well the enormous resources the rulers of the New Kingdom had at their command.

Akhetaten (modern Amarna), the creation of the 'heretic' pharaoh Akhenaten, is the best-preserved urban site in Egypt, thanks to the fact that it was cursed and no longer inhabited after Akhenaten's reign. Situated on the Nile's east bank 200km (125 miles) north of Thebes, Akhetaten occupied land that had never been dedicated to any god. Construction started early in Akhenaten's reign, and it was fully functional by his ninth regnal year. The city at its height stretched 9.6km (6 miles) along the Nile and had a population purposely brought there of 20,000–50,000. The city included enormous ceremonial buildings, including two royal palaces and two great temples to Aten, the god whose worship Akhenaten promoted. Carefully laid-out urban districts included gardens and pools for the wealthy and a large village for artisans. Many of the workers who built the city must have been forced to serve; excavation of the cemetery has shown the wretched condition of the poor, who suffered greatly from malnutrition and scurvy. Three-quarters of the adult bodies discovered had degenerative joint disease, suggesting years of carrying heavy burdens, and two-thirds had fractures. Many had died young.

The other great royal city of the New Kingdom was Piramesse, begun as a palace in the reign of Sety I, which Rameses II then expanded into a city that covered about 10.4 sq km (4 sq miles). It was a harbour town on the Pelusiac branch of the Nile, just downstream from the site of the former Hyksos capital of Avaris. Memory of Piramesse's construction is preserved in the biblical book of Exodus, which tells that a new Egyptian king afflicted the Hebrews who had lived in the Delta for centuries, forcing them to build the 'treasure cities' of Pithom and Raamses; the latter must have been Piramesse. Although what the Hebrews endured was corvée labour rather than enslavement, to judge from the evidence of Akhetaten, conditions were harsh. Piramesse was abandoned at the end of the Twentieth Dynasty. Little of it now remains, both because of wetter conditions in the north and since many of its monuments were later moved to the city of Tanis.

OPPOSITE: **Akhenaten, Nefertiti and their daughters worshipping Aten. The exaggerated features of the pharaoh are characteristic of the 'Amarna style' of art.**

To worship Aten, people needed to worship the royal family as the sole conduits to the god.

numbers of amulets and other objects that display plainly that the workers had continued their personal pieties without change. But even those whose daily worship was unaffected would have suffered in the economic crisis caused by confiscations and destruction of the great priestly estates, since they were major employers and distribution centres for the general populace. The upper classes, much more attuned to the state religion, by which the king was the chief intermediator between gods and humans, would have been much more impacted, besides losing many lucrative priesthoods. Indeed, Amenhotep III's vizier, Amenhotep-Huy, opposed Akhenaten's religious changes despite the overwhelming tradition of venerating the king. He was regarded at the time as a martyr, and a recent discovery has revealed that at least 60 later officials chose to be buried in the former vizier's tomb, associating themselves in death with this heroic figure.

Akhenaten built temples dedicated to Aten throughout Egypt, the largest of them all provocatively placed next to Amun's temple at Karnak. However, no real provision was made for anyone but the royal family to worship the newly prominent deity directly; instead, to worship Aten, people needed to worship the royal family as the sole conduits to the god. Therefore, it's not surprising that several large villas at Akhetaten had steles and cult statues of Akhenaten and his chief wife Nefertiti. Nor should it surprise that Akhenaten, perhaps imitating his father, appointed a high priest of himself.

Scholars have spilled a great deal of ink about the role of Queen Nefertiti in the religious reforms and government of what is known as the 'Amarna period' (from the site of Akhenaten's city) more generally. Tantalizing hints suggest that this non-royal woman, probably the daughter of the vizier Ay, was a prominent figure. She, along with her six daughters, is showcased in the art of the court, sharing worship of Aten with her husband. On the walls of the Aten temple at Karnak, she is even depicted smiting captives with a mace, a traditional representation for pharaohs, not for their consorts. But she disappears from the extant sources after Akhenaten's 12th regnal year. A leading theory is that, rather than dying or suffering disgrace, the heretic pharaoh took another unprecedented step, making Nefertiti his co-ruler, whereupon she adopted the name Neferneferuaten. Some even believe that Nefertiti succeeded her husband as pharaoh.

Meanwhile, the work of government continued. Clearly most officials continued to obey their pharaoh; there is no evidence of any widespread rebellion against his religious policy. Akhenaten himself travelled at times

OPPOSITE: **Bust of Nefertiti, discovered in an abandoned workshop in Amarna (the ancient Akhetaten).**

By Akhenaten's 12th year on the throne, rebellion was also brewing in Nubia, rebel leaders sensing a weakening of central oversight.

ABOVE: **One of the collection of Amarna Letters found in the ruins of Akhenaten's capital. Although it is a letter from King Abi-milku of Tyre to the pharaoh, it was written in the Akkadian lingua franca of the day and incised with cuneiform symbols on a clay tablet.**

OPPOSITE: **Head of Neferneferuaten Smenkhkara, Akhenaten's successor as pharaoh. Some scholars believe that 'he' was actually queen Nefertiti, continuing to rule after her husband's death.**

away from Akhetaten; he left instructions on the city's boundary stele that if he should die elsewhere his body should be brought back for burial. And modern scholars no longer believe that Akhenaten's supposed indifference to government precipitated a crisis in Egypt's far-flung empire. During Akhenaten's reign, Egypt controlled about 60 vassal city-states in Palestine and Syria. The evidence for neglect of his empire comes from the Amarna Letters, 382 cuneiform tablets written mostly in Akkadian, the lingua franca of the age. They constitute a royal archive, giving us a snapshot of international diplomacy. Some of the letters paint a dire picture, the prince of Damascus for example complaining that he has been left defenceless by the withdrawal of Egyptian troops. These letters should not be taken literally, however, as signs of a crisis because Akhenaten lost interest. They come from a world of petty rulers jockeying for position against their rivals and presenting the situation as darkly as possible in bids for favours. Egypt's peace treaties with both Mitanni and the Hittites also tied the pharaoh's hands. Still, Akhenaten seems at times to have been at least short-sighted, as when he chose not to intervene when Byblos begged for help against Hittite aggression. He also failed to retaliate when one of his own diplomats was murdered and the king of Amurru was implicated. Perhaps it is unsurprising that by Akhenaten's 12th year on the throne, rebellion was also brewing in Nubia, rebel leaders sensing a weakening of central oversight.

THE 'BOY KING' TUTANKHAMUN (1336–1327 BC)

Akhenaten's last recorded act dates to the 17th year of his reign; he probably died about then, as far as we know from natural causes. Egypt appears to have been in a state of some chaos by that point, exacerbated by the fact that Akhenaten did not have an adult son to succeed him. Unravelling the succession is complicated for modern scholars by the careful effort King Horemheb later made to eradicate all memory of the Amarna period. The heretic pharaoh's immediate successor was Neferneferuaten (1338–1336 BC)

who, because of the feminine form of part of the name is sometimes taken to be Nefertiti in a new role. Perhaps more likely, this pharaoh (also known as Smenkhkara) was a royal kinsman, perhaps Akhenaten's brother. He (or she) was succeeded by a nine-year-old boy, who soon changed his name from Tutankhaten to the more religiously acceptable Tutankhamun. DNA studies have demonstrated that Tutankhamun was the son of Akhenaten and Akhenaten's sister-wife, a figure for whom there is no historical record. That the son did not directly succeed the father drives home how precarious the governmental situation was at the time. When Tutankhamun *did* become pharaoh there was no queen to serve as regent, so instead a senior military official, Horemheb, took charge, apparently being declared heir presumptive at the same time. Tutankhamen's government began the restoration of traditional religion; the Restoration Stela from his reign describes Egypt's ruinous state and the threat to its armed forces abroad.

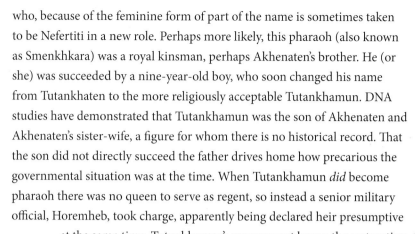

BELOW: Tutankhamun's Restoration Stela, in which the boy pharaoh proclaims a return to the worship of Egypt's traditional deities. It was probably erected in the fourth year of his reign.

Tutankhamun died in his tenth regnal year, probably before he ever actually ruled in his own name. Although sickly, with a painful, deformed left foot, the pharaoh's death was unexpected, perhaps from a head wound caused by a fall from a chariot. As a result, the boy king's burial was a rush job, the body placed in a tomb so small it must never have been intended for a king but that was complete and handy. Tutankhamun would rate barely a footnote in history had this tomb not been discovered by Howard Carter in 1922, one of only two pharaonic burials that have been found intact. The richness of the burial equipment for this insignificant ruler is stunning, including an inner coffin made of solid gold and weighing 110kg (243lb) – one can only imagine the extravagant burials of more fortunate pharaohs. Tutankhamun's tomb, although broken into twice shortly after his burial, was preserved by Maya, the overseer of the treasury, who also rescued the mummy of Akhenaten and other members of the royal family, reburying them at Thebes.

Tutankhamun's tomb included the embalmed foetuses of two girls, the daughters of Tutankhamun and his chief wife Ankhesenamun. But he died without heirs of his body. Horemheb, the designated heir (at

ABOVE: **Although denuded of the treasures with which he was originally buried, Tutankhamun's mummified remains were returned to his tomb in the Valley of the Kings in 2007.**

least by his own account) was probably campaigning against the Hittites at the time, so another senior official, Ay, seized the opportunity to declare himself pharaoh (1327–1323 BC). A peculiar story, preserved in a Hittite text, tells that Tutankhamun's widow Ankhesenamun was unwilling to accept the situation and wrote to the Hittite king Suppiluliumas I, asking him to send a son to marry her and rule Egypt. A prince was dispatched, but was murdered at the border, probably by Ay's agents. The elderly vizier-turned-pharaoh then married Ankhesenamun instead; he was probably Nefertiti's father and thus his bride's grandfather.

RELIGIOUS RESTORATION UNDER HOREMHEB (1323 TO 1295 BC)

It was Horemheb, however, who was really responsible for Egypt's restoration. He finally took the throne upon Ay's death. The new pharaoh took immediate steps to assert his right to the throne, including a campaign to deface and destroy the monuments of his rival Ay; even Ay's tomb was destroyed, and the sarcophagus smashed to pieces. A greater challenge was that Horemheb was a commoner from Herakleopolis, who had risen through the military ranks to command Tutankhamun's army. In the Coronation Text (found inscribed on the back of a statue), Horemheb laid out the case that he had a direct divine mandate. The text relates that Horus chose Horemheb to be king when he was

The 'Ramessid' period was an age of grandiosity and glitter, aptly called a 'gilded' age.

still a young man, a choice confirmed by Amun when Horus presented his favoured mortal to the greater god during the celebration of an *opet* festival. In practical terms, Horemheb must have won widespread noble support with his vigorous efforts to restore *maat* by reopening and repairing the temples, appointing new priests from among his army comrades. He attempted to erase the very memory of the Amarna period, dating his own reign from the death of Amenhotep III, destroying the heretic city of Akhetaten and defacing or usurping the monuments of his predecessors. Horemheb proved to be a strong ruler; the Great Edict found inscribed on a stela at Karnak tells how he cracked down on soldiers extorting from the populace and judges who took bribes.

THE DAWN OF THE 'RAMESSID' PERIOD

Horemheb had no son, but assured a smooth succession by naming his vizier and confidant as co-ruler and heir. The elderly Rameses I (1295–1294 BC) was thus able to move seamlessly to the throne, ushering in the Nineteenth Dynasty. He immediately named his son Sety as co-ruler. Thus began what is known

BELOW: **Detail from a wall painting of Horemheb with the goddess Nephthys in the pharaoh's well-preserved tomb.**

as the 'Ramessid' period. It was an age of grandiosity and glitter, aptly called a 'gilded' age. The rulers of the Nineteenth Dynasty, especially Rameses II, very blatantly displayed their greatness to the world, but it is hard to avoid the sense that they were trying too hard. Their vast narrations of victories hide the fact that their enemies were at least as strong as they were. Moreover, the image of godlike kings had been badly tarnished by this time, and Egypt's powerful elites needed to be convinced of the king's greatness. The necessity of working with a stronger, more vocal elite class had decisively shifted the balance of power.

The first four Ramessids – Rameses I, Sety I (1294–1279 BC), Rameses II (1279–1213 BC) and Merenptah (1213–1203 BC) – certainly set out to impress. Sety continued the restoration of temples damaged in the Amarna period, but also constructed a great temple at Abydos, at the supposed tomb of Osiris. Also, although the Nineteenth Dynasty continued to hide their tombs in the Valley of the Kings, Sety still thought big; his labourers cut about 91m (300ft) into limestone cliffs, and then decorated the passage and burial chamber with the finest reliefs and paintings of all the Theban royal tombs.

Many people's first thought of the great monuments of Egypt (after the pyramids) is of the massive structures of Rameses II's long reign. The first of these was his mortuary temple at Thebes, the Ramesseum. Dedicated to Amun and the deified Rameses II himself, the temple was a large complex that included a royal residence; an inscription at the sandstone quarry at Gebel

ABOVE: Interior of the temple of Sety I at Abydos.

el-Silsila reports that 3,000 workers cut stone there just for the Ramesseum. Colossal statues of the king, more than 16.8m (55ft) high, decorated the entrance. It was one of these colossi that inspired Shelley's sonnet 'Ozymandias', a corruption of Rameses' Horus name Usermaatra. Even more famous, though, are the twin temples constructed far to the south, near the modern village of Abu Simbel at the second cataract of the Nile. At the Great Temple, the seated colossi of the king stand a full 19.8m (65ft) high, with the rest of the edifice, cut into a cliff face, of similarly grand proportions. The entire Great Temple was cut from the cliff and relocated in 1964–1968 to save it from the waters of Lake Nasser after the Aswan High Dam was completed – a vast international effort. It is interesting to note that the Nineteenth Dynasty was also concerned to repair pharaonic monuments from the distant past. Khaemwaset, one of Rameses II's many sons, restored several Old Kingdom pyramids and copied the Old Kingdom style on some of his own monuments. All was not well, however. Buildings from the latter years of Rameses II's long reign (he was about 90 years old when he died) reveal economic decline, with use of recycled materials and increasingly shoddy techniques.

THREATS ON MULTIPLE FRONTS

Long gone were the days when Egypt was the uncontested powerhouse of the region. By the 13th century BC, the whole Mediterranean world was suffering from growing insecurity, and Egypt was not exempt. Sety I, already

RIGHT: An international recovery effort was needed to save Rameses II's temple at Abu Simbel from the waters of Lake Nasser. Crews cut the temple out of the cliff side in which it had been built and painstakingly re-erected it on higher ground.

an experienced general under Horemheb, had to deal with a newly significant
threat to the northwest. Several Libyan tribes, semi-nomadic pastoralists,
had begun to infiltrate Egypt's Delta, and were made more dangerous by
support from the pirate confederations that had begun to dominate the
Mediterranean. Sety contained the threat, but could not end it. He also had
to fight to the northeast, suppressing a rebellious confederation in Palestine
shortly after assuming sole rule; we are told that he marched 'like a fierce-eyed
lion'. The following year, he put down unrest in the Palestinian city-states,
and in two campaigns regained about half the territory that had been lost in
the Amarna period. The powerful Hittite Empire soon regained the territory
it had claimed, however, and the result was a stalemate, leaving Sety no real
option but to make a treaty with the Hittite king Muwatallis II.

For all his boasting of great victories, Rameses II had no greater success.
We have an extraordinary 13 extant Egyptian accounts of the Battle of Kadesh,
fought in his fourth regnal year, in 1274 BC. Rameses, commanding his own
army, was deceived by two nomadic scouts into thinking the Hittites were
still distant, and his army was thus caught by surprise. Only the pharaoh's
consummate leadership (so he claimed) saved the day. Although Rameses
presented the battle, including in great panels on the Ramesseum, as a great
victory, in reality it was another stalemate. After years of fighting, Rameses
II, like his father, gave up hope of defeating the Hittites and agreed to a

ABOVE: **Sety I driving his
war chariot, from the Great
Hypostyle Court at Karnak.
In reality, kings would have
had trained drivers (often an
adult son), but the artistic
convention was to present
the pharaoh alone.**

THE RAMESSID HAREM

While pharaohs had always been polygamous (unlike common Egyptians), the size of the royal harem grew enormously in the New Kingdom. Thutmose III established a royal harem retreat and retirement home in the Faiyum, and it must have seen much use as especially Rameses II cycled through numerous women, maintaining an establishment of perhaps as many as 200 at times in his reign. By the Nineteenth Dynasty, brother–sister marriage was no longer common, but a great royal wife still governed the harem, and her son was the preferred heir.

In the diplomatic world of the New Kingdom, treaties were often sealed by marriage to a foreign princess. Thutmose III and IV had a number of wives with Asian names, and clearly the custom of foreign marriages caught on well, as Amenhotep III's harem included two princesses each from Syria, Babylon, Arzawa and Mitanni. Such marriages were intended as displays both of friendship and of the greatness of the bride's birth country. When Princess Gilukhepa of Mitanni was sent to Amenhotep, she came with a 317-person strong entourage, as a scarab informs us. We also know that after Burna-Buriash II of Babylon sent a daughter to the same pharaoh, he was deeply offended that Egypt had dispatched only five carriages with the escort sent to collect her, insufficient for a woman of her standing. Egypt still maintained at least the facade of superiority, though, adamantly refusing to send its own princesses out for marriage to foreign rulers (one Asian ruler said he would take any Egyptian noblewoman, since he could pass her off as a princess). And only one foreign bride became the great wife, Rameses II's first Hittite wife, who had been sent to seal the treaty between Rameses and Hattusili III.

The byproduct of these large harems was an extensive royal family, which probably played a role in destabilizing the country in the Nineteenth Dynasty. Rameses II in particular was notable for his virility, boasting of more than a hundred sons (he did not enumerate the daughters). Modern Egyptologists think it likely that he actually had 48–50 sons and anywhere between 40 and 53 daughters.

LEFT: **Hinged Cuff Bracelet, New Kingdom, Eighteenth Dynasty (*c.*1479–1425 BC), from the Theban Tomb of the Three Foreign Wives of Thutmose III. Three pairs of hinged bracelets are associated with this tomb.**

OPPOSITE: **Hormin, the official who administered Sety I's harem, being rewarded for his services with gold necklaces on this limestone stela now in the Louvre.**

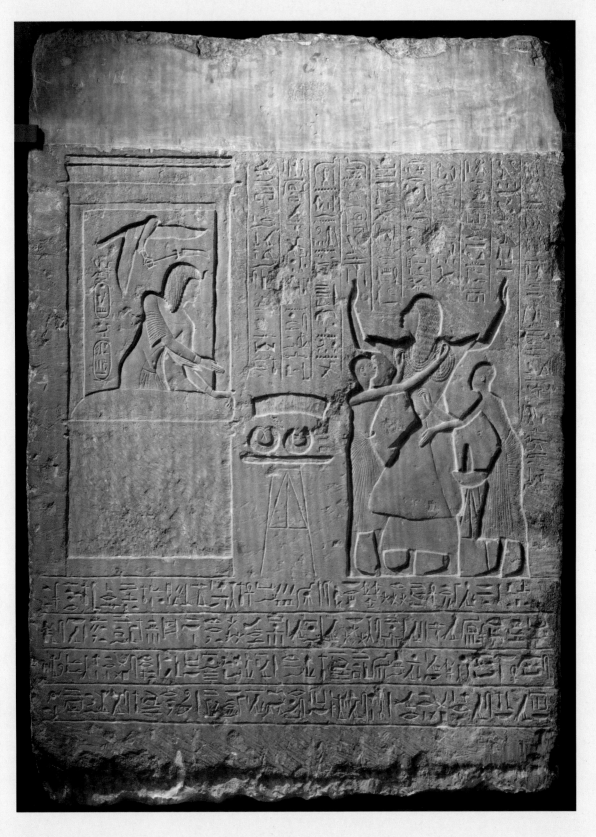

reign, he was probably more concerned with incursions from the northwest, constructing a string of fortresses in the northwestern Delta to contain the Libyan and pirate threat.

CONFUSION REIGNS

Too many sons could be a two-edged sword. Rameses II lived so long that it was his *13th* son who succeeded him, 12 heirs having predeceased their father. Merenptah (1213–1203 BC) was probably already in his 50s when he ascended the throne. Unsettled conditions in the Mediterranean were increasing pressure on Egypt. Most notably, in his sixth year, Merenptah had to face a double threat. First, a coalition of Libyans and 'Sea Peoples' – whole peoples on the move in the Mediterranean world – invaded the western Delta, probably driven by famine. Merenptah defeated them in a major battle, and a Karnak inscription reported more than 8,000 enemy dead and that the Libyan chief fled so quickly that he left his sandals behind. Almost immediately thereafter he had to suppress the revolt of a Kushite prince who had been in league with the Libyans, which he did so brutally (with public impalements and even burial alive of captives) that Egypt must have perceived the rebellion as a major threat. But then came confusion, probably caused by the enormous number of royal kinsmen. Merenptah's designated heir was Sety II, but his rule was contested by Amenmesse, a prince of the royal blood whose actual relationship to Merenptah has been endlessly contested. The result was a civil war between two rival pharaohs, and it took Sety II (1200–1194 BC) several years to triumph over his rival.

When Sety II died, the throne fell to Saptah (1194–1188 BC), a ten-year-old boy crippled by polio. The regency for the child was shared by his stepmother Tausret and the chancellor, a Syrian named Bay. Bay became very powerful, naming himself as 'great chancellor of the entire land' and even having the audacity to depict himself the same size as the king on reliefs. He fell from grace in Saptah's fifth year, though, and an ink memo written by a workman constructing Bay's tomb tells that the king killed 'the great enemy Bay'. Bay's demise left Queen Tausret the only power in the land, and when Saptah died in 1188, she took the throne in her own name. Her reign is obscure, and we are not even certain who she was. Tausret is never named as a king's daughter, but she was probably a descendant of Rameses II. She had been Sety II's chief wife, but their child together had died young. Tausret tried to present a strong image, including backdating her ascension year to the death of Sety II, but her reign lasted only two years. We do not even know if she died of natural causes or was deposed. Whichever the case, with her the Nineteenth Dynasty ended, and Egypt's greatest glory days were behind it.

DECLINE OR TRANSFORMATION?

A stela found at Elephantine reports that Sethnakht (1186–1184 BC) came to the throne because an oracle told that he had been sent by the gods to restore *maat* to Egypt. The new pharaoh further claimed that he took the throne 'to clear the land of traitors', suggesting that the ruling queen Tausret had been overthrown by force. He is known to have welcomed back officials who had fled the court in Tausret's reign. We do not know who this founder of the Twentieth Dynasty (1186–1069 BC) was, but he was probably related in some way to Rameses II. Tausret suffered the usual fate of unpopular rulers: her body was apparently denied honourable burial, and Sethnakht made himself at home in the tomb she had constructed for herself, covering Tausret's name on the walls with plaster so his own could be inscribed.

OPPOSITE: **In this relief from the tomb of Prince Amunherkepshef, the goddess Isis is depicted embracing the prince's father, Pharaoh Rameses III. Note how deity and ruler are portrayed as equals.**

RIGHT: **Head of a statue of Ahmose II, Twenty-sixth Dynasty (reigned: 570–526 BC). Greek historian Herodotus describes Ahmose as a shrewd ruler who promoted and controlled trade with Greece.**

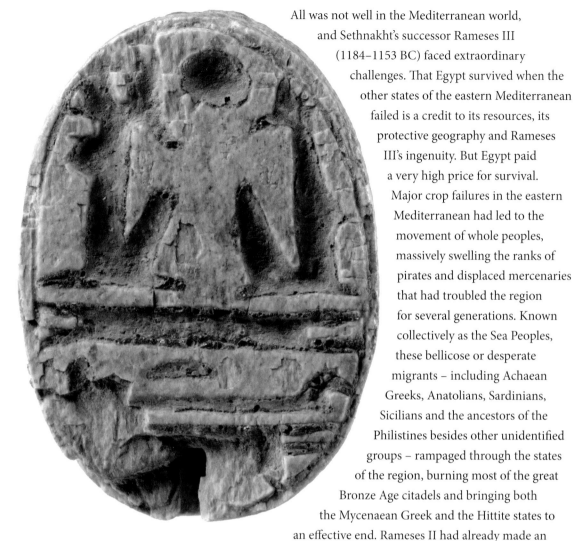

ABOVE: **Scarab inscribed with the name of Sethnakht, first pharaoh of the Twentieth Dynasty.**

All was not well in the Mediterranean world, and Sethnakht's successor Rameses III (1184–1153 BC) faced extraordinary challenges. That Egypt survived when the other states of the eastern Mediterranean failed is a credit to its resources, its protective geography and Rameses III's ingenuity. But Egypt paid a very high price for survival.

Major crop failures in the eastern Mediterranean had led to the movement of whole peoples, massively swelling the ranks of pirates and displaced mercenaries that had troubled the region for several generations. Known collectively as the Sea Peoples, these bellicose or desperate migrants – including Achaean Greeks, Anatolians, Sardinians, Sicilians and the ancestors of the Philistines besides other unidentified groups – rampaged through the states of the region, burning most of the great Bronze Age citadels and bringing both the Mycenaean Greek and the Hittite states to an effective end. Rameses II had already made an alliance with the Hittites against these Sea Peoples and Merenptah had defeated a wave that reached Egypt. Rameses III, however, had to face their main onslaught.

An extensive written account on a pylon of Rameses' temple at Medinet Habu – the longest known hieroglyphic inscription – gives a sense of how desperate Egypt's situation was and also of the pharaoh's intelligent strategy. Fortunately forewarned, Rameses ordered the fortification of the Nile's mouths. He then allowed the Sea People fleet to enter certain branches of the river, closing off the Nile once they had entered. The combined Egyptian navy and army thus trapped a number of enemy units, who were forced to fight piecemeal instead of deploying overwhelming force at one location. Whole Sea People contingents were destroyed. Survivors were impressed into Rameses' military or enslaved. The Pelset (from Crete) were even resettled on the eastern Mediterranean coast to control several cities and fortresses Rameses was able to seize in the wake of Sea People destruction; they became known to history as the Philistines.

Rameses also had to battle a Libyan coalition that perhaps was working in alliance with the Sea Peoples. Thus, although the Sea People threat had ended, the Libyan danger remained, and Rameses III fortified a number of temples to protect them from Libyan raiders. Still, after the wars of his first 11 years, Egypt once against enjoyed peace and at least superficial prosperity. But the wars had drained the state's resources, and thanks to the Sea People depredations, tribute from Egypt's Asian vassals had shrunk and trade routes were collapsing. Rameses III's ambitious building projects did not help, nor did his massive donations to temples. It is estimated that by his reign, the priesthoods controlled one-third of the arable land of Egypt. A series of low Nile inundations deepened the crisis, causing widespread famine. Rameses

BELOW: **This scene carved on the first pylon of Rameses III's mortuary temple at Medinet Habu shows the pharaoh in the traditional pose of smiting his enemies, while Amun looks on in blessing.**

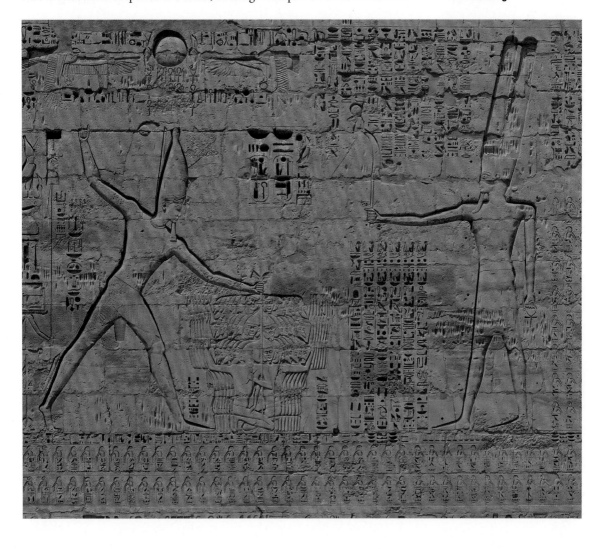

This modern illustration gives some sense of the chaotic Battle of the Delta in which Rameses III defeated the invading Sea Peoples

OVERLEAF: **The tomb of Rameses VI in the Valley of the Kings (KV9). Originally begun for his nephew Rameses V, Rameses VI simply took it over, enlarging the tomb and redecorating it. Fortunately, workers constructing this tomb built huts that concealed the entrance to Tutankhamun's tomb for more than 3,000 years.**

even had the dubious honour of the first known labour dispute in history. In the king's 29th year, the Theban tomb builders went on strike after their grain ration was not only late but also reduced. Shockingly, a vizier rebelled in the same year, making it plain that all was not well at the heart of government. Worst of all, the unimaginable happened: a plot formed against the ageing pharaoh and succeeded in assassinating him.

THE RULE OF SUCCESSIVE RAMESES

Rameses III is usually regarded as Egypt's last great pharaoh. After his death, king followed king in rapid succession – Rameses IV through XI only ruled a total of 84 years (1153–1069 BC). None of these ephemeral rulers left much of a visible footprint in Egypt. With no firm hand at the helm, the economic problems that plagued the country were worsened by rampant government corruption. Environmental stresses added even more to the problems, including the silting up of the Pelusiac branch of the Nile. There are references to famine and, in the reign of Rameses V, civil war. Rameses V himself fell ill in the major smallpox epidemic that killed six members of the royal family; the face of the pharaoh's mummy was painted with ochre to disguise the smallpox scars that had disfigured him.

A DOUBLE MYSTERY SOLVED

A text known as the Harem Conspiracy Papyrus reports the trial of a group of people accused of plotting to murder Rameses III. The defendants included Tiy, a minor wife who wanted her son to succeed to the throne, and a number of important palace officials and their wives. We are told that several of the plotters were executed.

Among those ordered to commit suicide was the prince the plot had supported, called by the pseudonym Pentaweret, 'He of the Great Female One', since his name had been cursed to oblivion. The papyrus does not tell whether the plot was successful or not. Add to that a second mystery: one of the mummies found in the Deir el-Bahri royal cache was discovered in a plain, uninscribed white case. The body was wrapped in ritually unclean sheepskin. Some natron had been pushed between the bandages wrapping the remains, but the young man's arms and legs were twisted, and his face distorted in agony. Could the 'Prince Unknown' be Pentaweret, Rameses III's would-be usurper, and had he possibly been buried alive as punishment?

It took modern forensic science to uncover the true outcome of the harem plot. The 'Prince Unknown' was indeed Rameses III's son, as DNA testing revealed. But he had not been entombed alive. The scientists investigating his remains found that the man, who was 18–20 years old at the time of death, had died from either strangulation or hanging, fitting with the suicide order mentioned in the papyrus.

Modern science also established that Rameses III was indeed assassinated. A CT scan of his remains in 2012 revealed that his throat had been deeply cut, severing the windpipe and major blood vessels; the embalmers had hidden the wound with a thick linen collar.

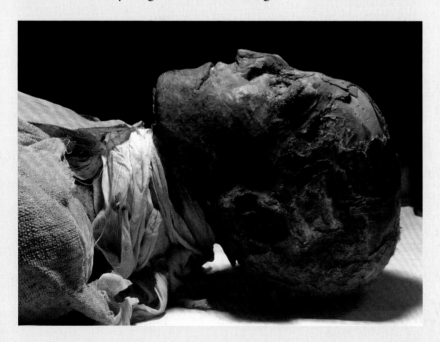

LEFT: **The mummified remains of Rameses III. Discovered in 1886, the pharaoh's final resting place is now the National Museum of Egyptian Civilization in Cairo, alongside four queens and 17 other kings.**

ABOVE: **A scene from the Great Harris Papyrus. This 42m (138ft)-long scroll is one of the longest papyri still extant from ancient Egypt. This panel depicts Rameses IV, accompanied by three deities.**

The central government's hold on the south gradually slackened, not just in Nubia but even in Upper Egypt. The last king to rule even weakly over Nubia was Rameses IX; as control had evaporated, the pharaohs of the Twentieth Dynasty lost access to the gold and other mineral wealth of the south. Even more ominous, though, was the loss of control over Upper Egypt, which since at least 3000 BC had been the powerhouse that had repeatedly unified the Egyptian state. With Rameses IV, the only clear engagement the pharaoh had with Thebes was to be buried there. A few years later, Rameses VI showed that he was incapable to defending the Theban area against Libyan raiders and Egyptian bandits.

It was the high priests of Amun in Thebes who filled the governmental vacuum in Upper Egypt. Indeed, it was probably their ever-growing power that displaced royal power in the first place. Already at the end of Rameses III's reign, the holdings of the Karnak temple were enormous. Papyrus Harris, dated to the day of Rameses III's death, tells that the temple employed a labour force of 81,322 and controlled 65 villages and the arable land that surrounded them, besides orchards, a massive amount of livestock, ships and workshops. They had the resources in Upper Egypt to provide peace and security for the

By his 19th regnal year, Rameses XI was a puppet.

common people, something the crown was increasingly unable to provide. By the reign of Rameses IX, the high priest Amenemope started asserting his power publicly, having his image not just carved on temple reliefs (which was itself a transgression) but as the king's equal. The kings of the late Twentieth Dynasty ruled from the north, largely leaving the south to the high priests of Amun in Thebes.

Finally, Rameses XI, the last member of the dynasty, seems to have given up government completely. He lived a reclusive life, leaving administration to courtiers. By his 19th regnal year, Rameses was a puppet. No clearer sign can be seen of royal breakdown than the spate of tomb robberies that began in the reign of Rameses IX and was renewed under Rameses XI. The robbers were not only rapacious but destructive – for example, burning mummies and smashing the massive granite sarcophagus of Rameses VI, which suggests active animosity towards the pharaohs. After Rameses XI made a general named Herihor high priest of Amun, Herihor soon took the final step of assuming royal trappings and the full titulary of a pharaoh, taking on independent rule of the south; General Smendes ruled the north.

BELOW: Herihor, high priest of Amun, here depicted as a king and being ritually purified by the gods Horus and Thoth. From the temple of Khonsu, part of the Karnak temple complex.

THE THIRD INTERMEDIATE PERIOD

Scholars since the 1960s have labelled the period after Rameses XI's death as a Third Intermediate Period; a common dating for it is 1069–664 BC. Once again, the unified state had broken down, so at times multiple dynasties claimed power simultaneously. To add to the confusion of the era, at least from a modern perspective, no king lists include the Twenty-first through Twenty-fifth Dynasties, so Egyptologists are forced to rely on the surviving excerpts of Manetho's history, eked out by evidence from the very small amount of royal building that took place before the mid-8th century BC. It was a period of foreign rule – by both Nubians and Libyans – while at the same time Egypt grew more inward-looking and reduced its dealings with the outside world. Paradoxically, however, the Third Intermediate Period demonstrates the strength of the pharaonic institution, as rulers claimed authority using symbols and rituals that were now over 2 millennia old. Still, times had changed, especially because there was no great drive to restore *maat* by reunifying Egypt; instead, peaceful federations of semi-independent rulers developed. A first sign of this is that Smendes quickly reached an agreement with the high priests who ruled the south, each side endorsing the other and Amun himself acknowledged as the ruler over both.

The Twenty-first Dynasty (1069–945 BC), which ruled in the north and exercised only a theoretical overlordship in Upper Egypt, saw the final dismantling of the New Kingdom royal burials at Thebes, at the order of Pinudjem, Amun's high priest and de facto ruler of the south. While inscriptions tell that the tombs were emptied and the kings' remains were removed to two royal caches to protect them from tomb robberies, it must have been stark financial necessity that drove the authorities to this step: by 1000 BC, Egypt was nearly bankrupt. Although the priests who opened the tombs treated the mummies with reasonable care, even rewrapping some, the kings were stripped of most of their valuables, which ended in the treasury

BELOW: Canopic jar inscribed with the name of Smendes, first ruler of the Third Intermediate Period. Canopic jars were placed in tombs to hold the internal organs of the deceased, which were removed during the mummification process.

of the general who ruled the south as high priest of Amun and occasionally claimed royal titles.

In the north, the rulers of the Twenty-first Dynasty did their best to keep up appearances. Smendes, the first pharaoh of the new dynasty (1069–1043 BC) married Rameses XI's daughter Tantamun to assert his link to the royal blood. He also established a new capital, moving from Piramesse to Tanis, the modern Sa'el Hagar in the western Delta. Tanis was largely rebuilt. But as Smendes and his successors could not afford art and architecture on the earlier scale, they adopted the simple expedient of moving many monuments of the Middle and New Kingdoms to the new capital, erasing the names on them and inserting their own. Still, they commanded wealth. The tomb of Psusennes I (1039–991 BC) was discovered at Tanis in 1940; it was very rich. It was hard to maintain the facade of godlike superiority, however, as can be seen when Siamun (978–959 BC), sixth pharaoh of the dynasty, allowed one of his daughters to marry a prince of Edom. Another of his daughters found herself in King Solomon of Israel's harem.

ABOVE: **The French archaeologist Pierre Montet (1885–1966) examining the sarcophagus of Psussenes I. In an extraordinary season of excavation, in 1939–40 Montet discovered the intact tombs of Psusennes I, Amenemope and Shoshenq II.**

THE ERA OF LIBYAN KINGS

Egypt's monarchy, supported by thousands of years of tradition, was strong, and the kings of the north regained the upper hand in the Twenty-second Dynasty (945–715 BC). There was, however, a startling new development: the rulers of this dynasty were of Libyan descent. The family of Sheshonq I (945–924 BC), founder of the new dynasty, had lived in the Delta for generations; there had been substantial Libyan settlement there ever since the time of Rameses II. The settlers had long become cultural Egyptians, but a sign of their ongoing 'foreignness' was that they still gave their children traditional Libyan names. Sheshonq before his ascension to the throne of Egypt was the acknowledged 'great chief of the Meshwesh', who served as the north's internal police force. He had also commanded Lower Egypt's armies, serving Psusennes II (959–945 BC). We do not know how Sheshonq came to the throne. It may well have been peaceful, his hold on power consolidated by marriage to Psusennes' daughter Maatkara.

Sheshonq was a strong ruler, asserting at least overlordship over all Egypt. One of the new pharaoh's moves to strengthen his authority was to install his younger son, Iuput, as high priest of Amun at Thebes, as well as governor of Upper Egypt. This move to limit the independence of the Theban high priests ultimately increased decentralization, however, establishing a junior branch of the royal line as a new power in the south that came to resent central control by the senior royal branch. In general, the heritability of administrative positions had become endemic by this time, senior bureaucrats, priests and military officers increasingly believing that they had a right to the positions their fathers had held, rather than receiving them as a gift from the pharaoh. These powerful local elites then intermarried, strengthening their hold on provincial centres.

It is not clear how much the Libyan pharaohs tried to fight the trend of decentralization, as long as they were recognized as suzerains. They had themselves depicted dressed like pharaohs, smiting Egypt's enemies before Amun and thus demonstrating their preservation of *maat*. They also continued to celebrate the *sed* festival; our best-preserved festival court is at Bubastis, built by Osorkon II (872–837 BC), fourth ruler of the dynasty. They also employed the full five-fold titulary of the pharaohs. But there was a significant change. Earlier kings had chosen titles as a programmatic

statement for their reign, while the rulers of the Twenty-second Dynasty simply copied earlier titles. Meanwhile, the Libyans apparently tolerated with equanimity the coexistence of several people with royal titles, non-royal people are shown performing royal functions and members of the royal retinue were even buried in royal tombs.

Sheshonq I, the Shishak of the Bible, was strong enough for Egypt to expand once again into western Asia. He launched a major campaign against Israel and Judah late in his reign; the account in the biblical I Kings says he came with 1,200 chariots and his troops included Libyans and Nubians. Sheshonq's troops sacked Jerusalem, carrying off the Temple and royal treasures. Since the triumphant king died soon afterwards, the victory was not followed up, and his successors were less ambitious.

BELOW: **Gold and lapis lazuli pendant depicting Osiris, Isis and Horus. It is inscribed with the name of Osorkon II of the Twenty-second Dynasty.**

OPPOSITE: **King Ahab of Israel battling the Assyrians at Qarqar (853 BC), as depicted by the great French artist Gustave Doré, one of 241 wood engravings he made for the *Bible of Tours*, published in 1843.**

After Sheshonq's rule and that of his son Osorkon I, most of the Libyan kings of the Twenty-second and Twenty-third Dynasty (818–715 BC) sink to insignificance. The years for which most of them ruled are unclear and Sheshonq IV was so unmemorable that modern scholars did not even notice his existence until the late 1980s. While the Libyan pharaohs held the north for nearly 400 years, the third ruler, Osorkon II, lost control of Upper Egypt. Osorkon allowed (or perhaps could not prevent) the installation of his cousin Harsiese as high priest of Amun in Thebes, and Harsiese soon declared himself pharaoh and independent ruler of the south. When Harsiese died, Osorkon was able to appoint one of his own sons to the high priesthood, but the trend towards decentralization continued. Still, Osorkon II cannot be regarded as weak. In this period, the Assyrian Empire was expanding into the Levant and Osorkon responded to the threat by joining a coalition of Israel and several small kingdoms to combat the Assyrian Shalmaneser III. They succeeded in stopping the Assyrian advance in 853 BC in the Battle of Qarqar.

By the later 8th century BC, the Libyan pharaohs had lost their hold on much of Egypt. Civil war raged between rival claimants in the south, and five different men calling themselves pharaohs ruled parts of Egypt. No faction seemed likely to gain the upper hand; the situation was clearly unsustainable. Egypt's return to stability came from an unlikely source, however, as yet again foreigners claimed the crown of Egypt. Only this time, rather than being long-term residents of the land, they took the throne by invasion from Nubia.

THE NUBIANS SEIZE POWER

When Egyptian rule receded from Egypt, it created a vacuum for the chieftains of Upper Nubia to reconstitute the Kingdom of Kush. By the mid-8th century BC, the chiefs of Napata had succeeded

in establishing their overlordship over all of Nubia; Kashta, the first king of Kush for whom there are contemporary records, was recognized as king as far north as Aswan. The upper classes of Nubia were highly Egyptianized after centuries of Egyptian rule and began to define themselves using the traditions of Egyptian kingship. Thus Ay, apparently the father-in-law of Egypt's eventual conqueror, had his name inscribed in a cartouche and was called the 'son of Ra' like an Egyptian pharaoh. Ay's successor as king of Kush, Kashta, is attested on an inscription found at Elephantine, where he named himself 'king of Upper and Lower Egypt'. It was Kashta's son Piy who actually invaded Egypt and made that boast a reality.

The Kushite Piy (747–716 BC) seized Upper Egypt in the first decade of his reign. He took Thebes without a fight, and the surrender or capture of other towns of the south was speedily accomplished. Piy consolidated his hold on Upper Egypt by arranging for the God's Wife of Amun – who by this time had become more influential than the high priest of the god – to adopt his own sister Amenirdis I as her successor. It is not clear if Piy took up residence in Egypt at this point or continued to reside in Nubia. But if he had returned to his homeland, Piy soon found it necessary to return to Egypt. The petty kings of the north – independent rulers of Tanis, Herakleopolis, Hermopolis and Leontopolis – feared the Kushites enough to band together against the common threat. Tefnakht, first of the two kings of the ephemeral Twenty-fourth Dynasty (727–715 BC), regained control of his city of Memphis, forcing Piy to respond. The coalition army met Piy in battle, only to suffer a significant defeat. Content to humiliate rather than kill his rivals, Piy allowed them to return to their home cities, as governors rather than kings. The Victory Stela Piy erected at his greatly expanded temple of Amun at Gebel Barkal was discovered in 1862. It is dated to Piy's 21st regnal year, so the campaigns in the north must have occurred in years 19 and 20. The stela depicts Egypt's provincial rulers prostrating themselves before Piy. The accompanying inscription, framed in traditional language and drawing on earlier models, is an expression of the ideal role of a king, with emphasis on Piy's justice and role in re-establishing *maat*.

The Victory Stela provides a valuable clue to how the Kushite kings of Egypt made their rule acceptable to their new subjects. Piy and his successors presented themselves as defenders of Egypt's gods and traditions from the beginning of their intervention in Egypt. When Piy reached Thebes in his

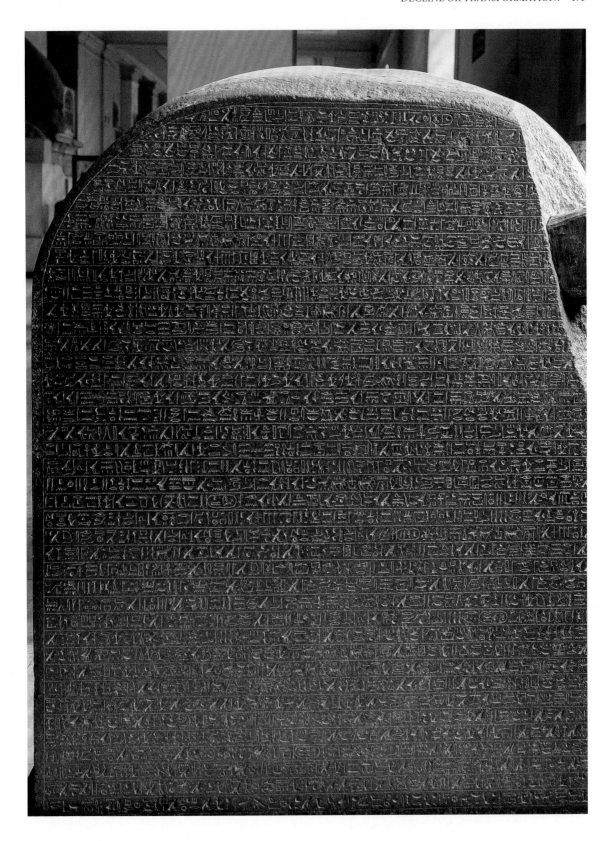

THE KUSHITE ROYAL TOMBS

ABOVE: **K-1 (Ku. 1) pyramid, El-Kurru near Karima, northern Sudan. The royal cemetery was the designated burial site not only for Kush pharaohs but also Egypt's 25th Dynasty.**

The Kushite pharaohs of the Twenty-fifth Dynasty were highly Egyptianized, but chose to be buried in their homeland. Their tombs provide fascinating clues about the way these rulers wanted to present themselves to the world. A first important point is that they chose to erect pyramids over their tombs, associating themselves in this way with the pharaohs of the Old Kingdom and the Twelfth Dynasty. Their pyramids were smaller than those of Egypt and built at a sharper angle, but still served as an important propaganda statement.

The main necropolis of the Twenty-fifth Dynasty was at el-Kurru in what is now Sudan, although late rulers chose to be buried at Nuri. Piy was interred there, in a tomb under a pyramid superstructure. His tomb, like others in the necropolis, is virtually indistinguishable from Egyptian

royal burials. The walls were painted with traditional Egyptian scenes and inscribed with hieroglyphs in the Egyptian language. The dead king was even provided with *shabti* figures, the small model servants intended to do any work demanded of the deceased in the afterlife.

Only two elements were unusual. First, the mummified remains were laid on a bed in the tomb rather than being enclosed in a sarcophagus, apparently following Kushite tradition. In another unusual feature, four chariot horses were buried in a standing position near the burial chamber, doubtless sacrificed to serve the king in death.

initial invasion, he publicly demonstrated his veneration
of Amun – and his claim to be more than a Kushite
chief – by celebrating the *opet* festival, in which the
pharaoh communed and mingled his essence
with that of the god. It is also striking that when
the Kushite king took Memphis by storm, he
sent troops to protect the city's temples. Piy
also associated himself with the great warrior
pharaohs of the New Kingdom by assuming
the Horus names of Thutmose III and
Rameses II.

THE SECOND KUSHITE CONQUEST

The north had soon reasserted its
independence, probably taking advantage of
Piy's return to Nubia. Piy's successor Shabaqo
(716–702 BC), who followed his brother on
the throne in 716 BC, soon invaded again; he
is often regarded as the first full ruler of the
new Kushite Dynasty, perhaps largely because
he established his capital at Memphis. He
may have employed greater violence in the
reconquest than Piy had in the first Kushite
onslaught, regarding the petty kings of the
north not just as rivals but as rebels. Although
many modern scholars doubt the story, two late
accounts tell that Shabaqo captured Bakenrenef (720–715 BC),
the second and last king of the Twenty-fourth Dynasty, and burned him alive.
Even if the tale is true, the new lord of Egypt soon showed himself willing to
work with local princes, allowing them to remain largely independent – as
long as they did not claim to be kings.

Shabaqo himself assumed the full titulature of a pharaoh and he and his
successors ruled both Kush and Egypt. Like his brother, Shabaqo presented
himself as a restorer of right order rather than as a conqueror. Shabaqo and
his successors Shabitqo (702–690 BC) and Taharqo (690–664 BC) all made
Memphis their chief residence in Egypt, building significantly there as well as
at Thebes. They also invested in the religious centres of other gods, including
the temple of Osiris at Abydos and impressive temples of Hathor at Dendera,
Khnum at Esna and Horus at Edfu. In addition, they all took care to associate
themselves with the great pharaohs of the Old Kingdom. A notable sign

**ABOVE: The Donation Stela of
Shabaqo. On it, King Shabaqo
offers the hieroglyph for 'field'
to the goddess Wadjet and the
god Horus, commemorating
a gift made to the temple of
Wadjet in Buto. The text is
mostly in the cursive style of
writing known as hieratic.**

The Kushite kings all took care to associate themselves with the great pharaohs of the Old Kingdom.

ABOVE: **Head from a statue of Pharaoh Shabitqo. The Nubian ruler has been sculpted following the canon for depictions of Egyptian kings, making no allowance for ethnic differences.**

of how interested the Kushite pharaohs were in maintaining ancient traditions is that Shabaqo was responsible for the preservation of the so-called Memphite Theology, a text that explains the creation of the world and the first creation of a united Egypt. Shabaqo ordered that the content of the damaged old papyrus with the account be reinscribed on stone. Although now hard to read since the stone was later used as a millstone, it reflects Kushite interest in linking their own rule with that of the great pharaohs of the distant past.

Herodotus, writing several centuries later, tells that Shabaqo had a reputation as a just ruler who was concerned for his people's well-being. His works included the construction of dykes to protect towns from the Nile's annual inundation. Nonetheless, the basis of Kushite rule was military might, and the whole of the Twenty-fifth Dynasty shows close links between the pharaoh and his army.

ASSAULT BY THE NEO-ASSYRIAN EMPIRE

The Kushite pharaohs did not simply decline, as the Libyan rulers had before them. Instead, the five kings of the Twenty-fifth Dynasty had to face the overwhelming might of the Neo-Assyrian Empire. In the course of the 8th and 7th centuries BC, this highly militaristic state became the largest empire the world had yet seen, pushing ever closer to Egypt and finally conquering it. That the Kushite pharaohs held out as long as they did is a testimony to the ongoing vitality of the Egyptian economy and the ability of its rulers to command its resources. Thoroughly alarmed by Shalmaneser V's conquest of Samaria and Sargon II's further thrusts into Syria, Shabaqo had taken to the battlefield to oppose the Assyrian advance, but was defeated in the Battle of Raphiah in 217 BC. Shabaqo's successor Shabitqo then joined an alliance of small kingdoms hoping to take advantage of the death of Sargon II to stop the Assyrians' inexorable spread, but they

The Roman historian Strabo says that Taharqo was one of the greatest military tacticians of antiquity.

too were defeated, at the Battle of Eltekeh in 701 BC. The Assyrian ruler Sennacherib then pushed on into Egypt, but was defeated and withdrew.

It is not clear how the Kushite succession functioned. The fourth pharaoh of the dynasty was Taharqo, whose father was almost certainly Piy. Taharqo had lived in Nubia until he was about 20 years old, after which Shabitqo had summoned him to Egypt. He inherited the throne at the age of 25, and ruled for 26 years. With some justice, the Roman historian Strabo says that Taharqo was one of the greatest military tacticians of antiquity. Ably supported above all by Mentuemhet, the prince of Thebes, Taharqo resisted the overwhelming power of the Assyrians for years, and even when defeated refused to give up the fight.

The Assyrian Esarhaddon firmly controlled the Levant by about the year 677 BC, and was probably correct in blaming Egypt as the cause of continuing unrest there. Taharqo did in fact actively work to rally resistance to the Assyrians in the states he still hoped would provide a buffer for Egypt, including active support of the Phoenician city-states that had banded together to fight Esarhaddon. Esarhaddon invaded Egypt in 674 or 673 BC only to be defeated by the warrior pharaoh. Honour of course demanded that the Assyrian avenge such a slight, so a major Assyrian army followed up with a second invasion of Egypt in 671 BC. Assyrian sources tell that Esarhaddon battled Taharqo three times in the course of 15 days, the Assyrian army gradually driving the Egyptian and Kushite army back to Memphis. Taharqo was himself in the thick of the fighting and was forced to flee south after being wounded. Esarhaddon proceeded to take Memphis in a bloody assault; when the city fell, his captives included most of the royal court, including Taharqo's wives, sons and daughters, who were all carried off to Nineveh. The Assyrians marvelled at the amount of treasure they gathered while looting Memphis, including 16 tiaras and 30 other items of headgear for the royal women, which must have whetted their appetite for further conquest.

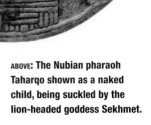

ABOVE: The Nubian pharaoh Taharqo shown as a naked child, being suckled by the lion-headed goddess Sekhmet.

With their king in Nubia, most Egyptians appear to have submitted to Assyrian rule. Never particularly understanding of the customs of other lands, the Assyrian king installed Assyrian officials and ordered offerings to the Assyrian gods in Egypt's temples; the cities along the Nile were given new Assyrian names, although mostly left under local administrators. Only the native prince of Sais, who had always been the main Egyptian opponent to Kushite rule, was reinstated.

After Esarhaddon withdrew, Taharqo soon returned to Egypt, only to be forced to retreat to Nubia once again in 669 BC when Esarhaddon's successor Ashurbanipal brought an army into Egypt yet again. The princes of Lower Egypt, unwilling to accept Assyrian rule, began plotting to restore Taharqo as soon as Ashurbanipal had withdrawn. In yet another attack, however, the Assyrians killed most of the princes, leaving only their Saite collaborator, Nekau, in place. That was the end of the story for Taharqo, who apparently gave up hope of reconquering Egypt. But his successor, the Kushite pharaoh Tanutamani (664–656 BC) made another attempt to drive out the Mesopotamian foreigners; he told on a stela at Gebel Barkal that he had a dream in which two serpents offered him the thrones of both Egypt and Nubia. Unfortunately, the divinely sent snakes had lied. Tanutamani regained Aswan, Thebes and even Memphis from the Assyrians, then defeated the Delta princes who had given at least some support to Assyria. But Ashurbanipal soon responded, rapidly retaking Memphis and then moving on to Thebes, sacking it and claiming the great temple treasure. Tanutamani was forced to retreat again to Nubia. Nonetheless, his resistance finally taught the surviving Egyptian princes the need for military and civil co-operation, paving the way to reunification of Egypt under Psamtek I of Sais (664–610 BC), whose father Nekau had been killed by Tanutamani.

THE SAITE RENAISSANCE

The Twenty-sixth, or Saite, Dynasty (664–525 BC) did not get off to a very promising start, although soon its reunification of all Egypt ushered in what is known as the Late Period (664–332 BC) of pharaonic history. Nekau I, the petty king of Sais in the Delta, had been an Assyrian client; his son Psamtek I inherited Assyrian support. But Psamtek proved to be a dynamic ruler, especially as Assyria's hold on Egypt was never very strong and, thanks to their brutal approach to rule, their kings usually had to combat enemies closer to home. Psamtek at first controlled about half of the Delta, soon expanding his rule to the entire Delta. Skilled diplomacy won him the support of Lydia in claiming independence from the Assyrians, who withdrew after suffering a defeat. Then, employing a combination of diplomatic and military means,

LEFT: Hutchinson's History of the Nations (1915) captures well the glory and power of the Assyrian king Esarhaddon in his capital city of Nineveh.

The red granite sarcophagus of Princess Nitocris of the Twenty-sixth Dynasty, discovered at Deir el-Medina.

Psamtek proceeded to extend his reach to include all of Egypt, a goal he accomplished by 656 BC. Particularly notable was Psamtek I's use of foreign mercenaries, especially Ionian Greeks, whose heavy body armour gave them a distinct advantage over most troops of the eastern Mediterranean and beyond. Diplomacy, too, played a role, however. The pharaoh's most decisive step to gain control of Upper Egypt was when he convinced the God's Wife of Amun in Thebes to adopt his daughter Nitocris as her heir. Then, as Theban officials died, he painstakingly placed people loyal to himself in their place.

What followed was a final flowering of Egypt under a native dynasty. The Saite era was marked by a return to stability and traditional religious values. It was also a true renaissance, a conscious looking back to the Old and Middle Kingdoms for inspiration in art as well as governance. The Saite pharaohs were careful to stress their connection to Egypt's history and their own Egyptian origins in both image and language. Their restoration of *maat* included repair of ancient monuments, such as the pious restoration of the tomb of the Fourth Dynasty ruler Menkaura. Besides restorations, the Saites also engaged in much new temple building. Unfortunately, the edifices of their dynasty are poorly preserved because they built mostly on the Delta, where wetter conditions over the millennia have destroyed multiple monuments and submerged many others. The pharaohs of the era also reinforced traditional religious practices, especially encouraging a new efflorescence of sacred animal cults.

What followed was a final flowering of Egypt under a native dynasty.

FACING DOWN FURTHER THREATS

Nekau II, who succeeded to the throne in 610 BC, continued his father's dynamic approach to rule. This included an element of military opportunism. Nekau II took advantage of Assyria's decline to seize control of Israel and Judah, which he held for about four years. But the power that finally brought down Assyria – Babylon – soon flexed its muscles in the Levant. In 605 BC, Nekau suffered a major defeat in the Battle of Carchemish, and was forced to retreat to Egypt. The Babylonian Nebuchadnezzar II soon followed, but in 601 BC Nekau succeeded in driving the Babylonian army back from the border of the Delta. Not for the first (or last) time, Egypt's geography helped save her from foreign invasion.

In this environment of successive Near Eastern empires, their rulers eager to gain the wealth of Egypt, Nekau II was farsighted enough both to take active steps to increase his revenue and to win new allies. Unlike most earlier Egyptian rulers, he fully recognized the possibilities of the sea, both for war and for peaceful trade. He had triremes built for expeditions on both the Mediterranean and the Red Sea, also forming an Egyptian navy with the

BELOW: Modern illustration of the Battle of Carchemish, fought in 605 BC between Egypt and her allies against the Babylonians.

aid of Ionian Greeks who had been displaced in the constant fighting of the Greek world. Herodotus tells that Nekau even commissioned a flotilla of Phoenician ships to attempt a circumnavigation of Africa; the purpose of such a venture, besides scientific curiosity, must have been to open up new trade routes. Above all, Nekau II was responsible for the digging of a navigable canal between the Nile and the Red Sea. Nekau's canal greatly facilitated trade with the eastern coast of Africa and was in use for centuries, repaired and deepened by later Persian and Ptolemaic rulers of Egypt.

The pharaohs of the Eighteenth Dynasty had shaped their image as Egypt's saviours from the depredations of the Hyksos, and the Saite kings appear to have done the same, trying to expunge the 'dishonour' of the period of Kushite rule. Psamtek II (595–589 BC) conducted a major campaign against Nubia in his third regnal year, employing two army corps – one native and the other composed of foreigners, mostly Jews and Greeks – for the purpose. The expedition penetrated at least as far south as the Nile's fourth cataract. Not content with defeating the king of Kush, Psamtek II also ordered the monuments of the Kushite pharaohs within Egypt defaced, erasing their names just as the Eighteenth Dynasty had done with the Hyksos.In their proper place, though, the Saite pharaohs had no objection to foreigners. Ionian Greeks, Carians and other mercenaries formed the backbone of the new Egyptian army. Many foreigners also settled in Memphis and throughout Egypt, sometimes housed in long-term camps as a military reserve, sometimes simply coming to take advantage of trade opportunities. It was probably to accommodate their needs that the Saite pharaohs introduced the relatively new invention of coinage.

It was impossible, however, to ignore foreign threats and possible opportunities. Military overreach in time led to the downfall of Apries (589–570 BC), the next Saite ruler. Apries supported Zedekiah of Judah, sending troops in an attempt to end Nebuchadnezzar II's siege of Jerusalem. But the Egyptian force was defeated and Apries could not prevent Jerusalem's fall in 586 BC, although he did give refuge to many Jews. The pharaoh enjoyed some military success, including several naval victories as he defended Egypt's commercial interests in Tyre and Sidon. However, he made a serious error when the king of Libya asked for help against Cyrene's expansion into his territory. Apries sent troops, choosing to employ native Egyptians rather than his Greek mercenaries. The Egyptian expeditionary force suffered a humiliating defeat at Irasa, and the survivors came home enraged at what they regarded as royal bungling. Apries sent a general, Amasis, to pacify the troops, but Amasis instead went over to the side of the rebels and declared himself pharaoh. Apries tried to take his throne back from the usurper with the help of Nebuchadnezzar II but was defeated and killed.

THE FIRST PERSIAN PERIOD

The usurper Amasis, also known as Ahmose II (570–526 BC), enjoyed a long and successful reign. He remained dependent on Greek mercenaries, but soothed Egyptian sensibilities by restricting Greek merchants to the city of Naucratis. Still, he was careful to make friends among the Greeks, including a massive donation for the restoration of Apollo's temple at Delphi. Amasis undertook a careful reform of the government, including the administration's shift to the simplified demotic writing system instead of the hieratic script that had been in use for centuries. Throughout his reign, Amasis did everything possible to shore up Egyptian power, expanding commerce in the eastern Mediterranean and conquering Cyprus. Above all, he supported anyone who opposed the rising power of the Persian Empire.

Amasis' moves against Persia were successful for his lifetime, but his successor had to bear the full brunt of Persian resentment. Psamtek III (526–525 BC), the last ruler of the Twenty-sixth Dynasty, did not last long on the throne. Almost immediately, the Persian king Cambyses invaded Egypt. Psamtek's army was defeated at Pelusium in 525 BC. The pharaoh himself escaped and fled to Memphis, but he was soon captured and taken to the

ABOVE: The Saite pharaoh Apries in battle. In reality, war chariots had not been used on battlefields for nearly half a millennium by the time Apries reigned in the 6th century BC.

OPPOSITE: This finely carved statue of Pharaoh Psamtek II now stands in the Louvre. Although Psamtek ruled only six years, a number of his buildings and statues have survived.

THE MURDER OF THE APIS BULL

Among the numerous oracles of Late Period Egypt, that of the Apis bull was perhaps the most venerated. Apis (in Egyptian, Hapi) was a physically incarnate deity, a son of Hathor born as a bull calf from a virgin cow that had been impregnated by the god Ptah. The calf was painstakingly cared for in Memphis, dressed in golden robes, and was believed to have oracular powers. When a senior bull died, it was mummified and buried with honour, and the priests of Apis would search for a new calf with the distinctive sacred markings.

Herodotus reports a story, certainly learned from Egyptian priests, that Cambyses after his conquest stabbed the sacred Apis bull, a horrible sacrilege that marked the Persian king as a 'criminal lunatic'. The reality is more complicated. Cambyses had been inspired in his conquest at least in part by desire for Egypt's wealth, and among other measures he cut deeply into temple revenues. As a result, the priests labelled him a transgressor and propagated stories intended to turn Egyptians against their conqueror.

In reality, Cambyses was very careful to avoid offending Egyptian sensibilities. He actually officiated at the burial of an Apis bull shortly after his arrival in Egypt, and also honoured the goddess Neith at Sais. He also presented himself as an Egyptian pharaoh, assuming the royal titulary and working with native Egyptians in his government. The only 'transgressive' act he is known to have performed was an intensely political one: he had the remains of the adamantly anti-Persian pharaoh Amasis exhumed and dismembered.

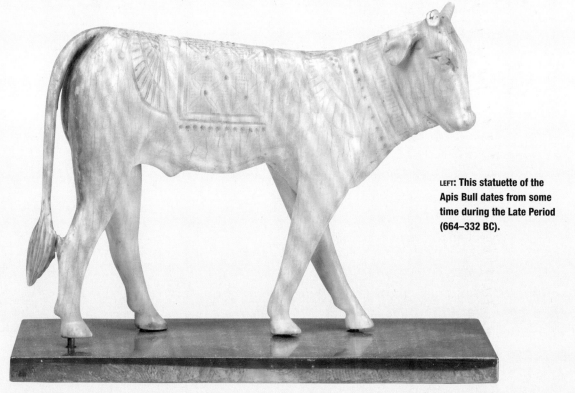

LEFT: **This statuette of the Apis Bull dates from some time during the Late Period (664–332 BC).**

ABOVE: **The meeting of Persian king Cambyses II and the Egyptian Psamtek III, as painted by the French artist Jean Adrien Guignet (1816–1854).**

Persian capital of Susa. At first accorded honourable treatment, he was soon suspected of treachery and executed. Cambyses himself was recognized as the king of Egypt (525–522 BC), and the first period of Persian rule is reckoned as the Twenty-seventh Dynasty (525–404 BC).

Egypt had been ruled by foreigners before, but the Persians were fundamentally different, both because they were Zoroastrians who did not actually believe in the deities of Egypt and because they were not resident in Egypt. Egypt had become a mere province of a greater empire, ruled by a satrap sent from Persia.

There may have been attempts to put a better face on this development. Turning again to Herodotus, we find the peculiar and unlikely story that Cambyses was Cyrus the Great of Persia's illegitimate son, the child of an Egyptian woman named Nitetis who was the daughter of the Saite pharaoh Apries. If this story had been true, Cambyses would have been half Egyptian and the Egyptian royal bloodline would have been transmitted to his children. Perhaps the story originated in an Egyptian attempt, like that which later invented Egyptian heritage for Alexander the Great, to make the reality of Persian rule more palatable.

It is not clear what Egyptians thought about rule by the culturally alien Persians. When circumstances were favourable, rebellions arose, but they were

ABOVE: **Making the best of foreign invasion, an Egyptian artist has depicted the Persian king Darius I as a traditional pharaoh making an offering to Anubis, with Isis standing behind. One panel of a box containing statuettes.**

usually limited to the western Delta. One rebellion, when Cambyses died in 522 BC, was soon suppressed by the new king Darius (522–486 BC). Darius visited three times and showed considerable interest in Egypt, maintaining religious sites and constructing a large new temple at the Khargah Oasis. Darius was depicted there as a traditional pharaoh. He also codified Egypt's laws, part of an empire-wide project, and restored the Egyptian educational system in many districts. He even completed or improved Nekau II's canal between the Nile and the Red Sea. At least some people regarded him as a traditional pharaoh, such as an old scribe who petitioned Darius for redress for wrongs done his family for more than a century; we don't have Darius' response. Nonetheless, Egypt rebelled after the Greek victory at Marathon in 490 BC. Darius set out to punish the rebels, but died before he could do so.

Xerxes (486–465 BC) brutally brought the Egyptians to heel, but Egypt remained restive under his rule, probably at least in part because Persia's new king did not bother to assume the traditional titles and duties of a pharaoh. A large-scale rebellion broke out in 460 BC after years of oppression by a rapacious governor, led by the Egyptian prince Inaros with support from Athens. The new Persian king, Artaxerxes I (465–424 BC), took a horribly punitive revenge, devastating whole regions and crucifying Inaros after he was captured. After a few years of peace, the accession of Darius II in 424 BC was marked by further rebellion. Finally, yet another rebellion began in late 405 BC. Its leader, Amyrtaios (404–399 BC), claimed royal status; he succeeded in driving out the Persians in the disorder after Darius II's death and is counted as the only ruler of the Twenty-eighth Dynasty.

THE DWINDLING OF EGYPTIAN RULE

The Twenty-ninth and Thirtieth Dynasties (399–343 BC) maintained a precarious independence from Persia, stripping Egypt's wealth to pay large numbers of Greek mercenaries. The period was unstable, with several usurpations suggesting that traditional veneration of the pharaoh had crumbled and that no ruler had unquestioned legitimacy. Nectanebo I (380–362 BC) did succeed in halting a massive Persian invasion in 373 BC, but only thanks to poor planning and dissension among the Persians. Teos (362–360 BC) was so unpopular because of the high taxes he demanded to pay for defence that his cousin Nectanebo II (360–343 BC) challenged him for the throne; Teos ended up taking refuge at the Persian court. Although the second Nectanebo fought skillfully against the Persians both militarily and diplomatically, Artaxerxes III (343–388 BC) successfully invaded Egypt in 343 BC. Nectanebo was forced to flee. Egypt did not see another native Egyptian ruler until AD 1952, 2,300 years later.

BELOW: This powerful statue of Nectanebo II, the last native pharaoh, standing under the protection of Horus in his hawk form, sums up well the ongoing strength of royal iconography even into the fourth century BC.

THE END OF INDEPENDENT EGYPT

It was perhaps inevitable that Egypt would in time fall into the hands of a Greek dynasty. After all, Hellenic influences had started to penetrate Egypt as early as the 7th century BC, and the pharaohs of the Late Period depended ever more on the support of Greek mercenaries. But it is unlikely that anyone could have anticipated the dramatic transformation of the Mediterranean and Middle Eastern lands wrought by Alexander the Great of Macedon. His reign propelled Egypt into a new world of Greek cultural influences and intensive rivalry for power among the descendants of Macedonian generals, with profound effects on the land of the Nile.

OPPOSITE: **Detail from the painting 'Cleopatra on the Terraces of Philae' by Frederick Arthur Bridgman (1896). The queen depicted is of course Cleopatra VII, the only Ptolemaic queen familiar to most people.**

RIGHT: **This very fine fragment from a large statue is attributed to the pharaoh Ptolemy II, or perhaps Ptolemy III or possibly to a high official of those reigns (285–246 BC). The fleshy features reflect an early influence of Hellenistic art on Egyptian styles.**

Alexander succeeded his father as king of Macedon in 336 BC when he was only 20 years old. Philip II had provided a substantial foundation for military expansion, building Macedon into a strong state with impressive military capability. He had also forced most of Greece's other states into an alliance with the goal of liberating the Greek cities of Asia that were subject to Persian rule. Alexander continued that dream, invading the western reaches of the Persian Empire and gradually working his way down the eastern seaboard of the Mediterranean, during which he won notable victories against superior Persian forces. In 332 BC, Alexander and his army marched on Egypt, whose people were suffering under the harsh rule of the second Persian period. The Egyptians were inclined to hail the Macedonian king as a liberator, and the Persian governor put a good face on the matter and welcomed the conqueror as well, since he did not have sufficient troops for resistance.

Alexander, always respectful of foreign customs, did everything possible to ensure Egyptian loyalty. He went to Memphis, the traditional site where the high priest of Ptah crowned pharaohs, and was acclaimed as pharaoh there. Even if the temple reliefs depicting his coronation were a later rationalization of the Macedonian's rule, Egypt's new lord certainly sacrificed to the Egyptian gods in Memphis, exercising a prerogative reserved to royalty. Alexander also identified himself as the son of the god Amun in the most striking way possible, journeying to the great oracle of Amun at Siwah to win recognition of his godhood.

The choice of Siwah rather than the great temple of Amun at Thebes was a brilliant stroke, since Amun at Siwah was already closely identified with the Greek Zeus, so the Siwah pronouncement added legitimacy to Alexander's claims in the Greek world, rather than just in Egypt. Perhaps it was still during his lifetime that a rumour spread that Alexander was the son of the last native pharaoh, Nectanebo II, or perhaps had been begotten by the god acting through the mortal king. The story as it developed by the time the *Alexander Romance* was written in the 2nd century AD tells that when Nectanebo fled the Persians he escaped to Macedon. A mighty magician, he was able to transform himself into a snake and fathered Alexander on Queen Olympias.

ABOVE: **Marble bust of Alexander the Great, one of many copies of the statues Lysippus made of the great conqueror during his lifetime.**

In his brief time in Egypt, Alexander certainly exerted every effort to consolidate his rule. Upon assuming the Egyptian crown, the new pharaoh took the Horus name 'protector of Egypt'; his other throne titles included 'he to whom the office of his father was given' and 'the one whom Amun chose'. Alexander also assured that the people would see Amun's approval. He rebuilt the ship shrine at the temple of Luxor so he could undergo the ceremony of being confirmed by Amun at the *opet* festival. The Macedonian also restored sacred bulls to their shrines and clearly gave orders that Egyptian sacred spaces should be respected; Peukestas, Alexander's commander in Memphis, issued an order to that effect.

Alexander the Great soon left Egypt again to pursue his conquest of the Persian Empire, but not before he had undertaken another act with long-term consequences for Egypt: he founded the city of Alexandria on the coast of the western Delta, on the site of the small New Kingdom town of Rhakotis. The creation of this major port city at an ideal location for trade assured that Egypt would look towards the Mediterranean more than ever before. The city grew rapidly and became by far the most important centre of Greek life and influence in Egypt.

THE HELLENISTIC AGE

If Alexander had left a clear succession, Egypt would doubtless have ended, as it had been under Persian rule, as a single province of a far-flung empire, ruled by an absentee monarch. Fate intervened, however. Alexander died in 323 BC, leaving a pregnant wife but no clear heir. Alexander's generals remained loyal to his dynasty for a surprisingly long time, first acclaiming as king their hero's mentally challenged half-brother Philip Arrhidaeus, and then ruling the various regions of the new Macedonian Empire as regents for Alexander's posthumous son Alexander IV. In the course of little

OVERLEAF: Ruins of the temple of Amun at the Siwah Oasis. Although deep in the western desert, both Egyptians and Greeks travelled to the temple for centuries to consult the oracle there.

BELOW: 'Alexander the Great at Memphis', by André Castaigne, part of a series of 36 scenes from the conqueror's life that Castaigne produced in 1898–99.

ABOVE: **Coin of Ptolemy I Soter and his third queen, Berenice. Like many women of the Ptolemaic dynasty, Berenice played an active political role.**

more than a decade, however, tensions had risen to the point that one of Alexander's former commanders murdered the boy king (and the youth's grandmother, Alexander's mother Olympias) and the rivalry to win rule over Alexander's conquests broke out with full force. It is a period known to history as the Hellenistic Age, as Macedonian generals and their descendants controlled lands that reached at times even into India, spreading Greek culture and administration over an enormous territory.

THE PTOLOMAIC DYNASTY (304–30 BC)

One of the chief beneficiaries of the rivalry between the 'Successors' was Ptolemy, son of Lagos. One of Alexander's most trusted commanders, Ptolemy had controlled Egypt since the death of Alexander, and when Alexander's son was murdered, he was acclaimed king by the resident Macedonian army. Ptolemy was crowned as pharaoh of Egypt on January 12 304 BC, the anniversary of Alexander the Great's death. Thus was born the Thirty-first or Ptolemaic Dynasty, Egypt's longest lasting and final period of dynastic rule.

Ptolemy I Soter (304–285 BC) shaped the course Egypt would follow for the next two and a half centuries with the decisions he made as he consolidated his hold on the land of the pharaohs. First and foremost, Ptolemy staked his claim to the throne on his supposed relationship to Alexander, rather than to any Egyptian native dynasty; although he married a daughter of Nectanebo II, he soon repudiated her in favour of a Greek marriage alliance. Instead, Ptolemy claimed to have Macedonian royal blood flowing in his own veins, circulating the story that he was an illegitimate son of Philip II and thus Alexander's older half-brother. In a major coup, he also gained possession of Alexander's body, creating the myth that the conqueror had desired his final resting place to be in Alexandria, which had become Ptolemy's own capital.

UNITING EGYPTIAN AND GREEK CULTURAL TRADITIONS

Ptolemy was intelligent enough to learn from the experience of earlier foreign dynasties. Although the Ptolemies never fully adopted Egyptian culture as had the Libyan and Nubian rulers of the Third Intermediate Period, they did have two important advantages compared to the Persians: they were resident in Egypt and they were polytheists. While the Zoroastrian Persians had for the most part shown respect for Egypt's gods, their dualistic religion made it impossible for them to engage in the rituals of worship that were so

BRINGING ALEXANDER 'HOME'

When Alexander the Great died in Babylon in 323 BC, plans were immediately made to return his remains to Macedon for burial in the royal necropolis at Pella. His body was carefully embalmed, and a sumptuous funeral cortege was organized. It began the long journey, but Ptolemy intercepted and diverted it to Egypt.

Apparently, he originally planned to take Alexander's remains for burial at the Siwah Oasis or in Memphis, but the Ptolemies finally settled on Alexander's own city of Alexandria. Construction began of an impressive mausoleum, known as the Soma, within which Alexander's embalmed body rested, enclosed in crystal so visitors could view it. Alexander was declared a state god and a purely Greek cult was established with a Greek priest at its head; no native ever held the office. The mausoleum itself was so elaborate that it took a century to complete.

We do not know what became of Alexander's tomb. Visitors came for centuries to marvel at his remains, including the future Roman emperor Augustus Caesar (who declined to pay his respects at the tombs of the Ptolemies in the same building). However, no source tells of its destruction. Most likely, the Soma was stripped of its gold adornments either when Christianity came to dominate Egypt or during the Islamic invasion of the 630s. There is a tradition that the Mosque of Nabi Daniel in central Alexandria was built over the Soma, but no trace of the Hellenistic building has been found. Most likely, Alexander's tomb is now under the waters of the Mediterranean, as is much of the ancient city of Alexandria.

LEFT: 'Augustus before the Tomb of Alexander the Great', by Sébastien Bourdon (1616–1671).

central to the pharaoh's role. Greeks, by contrast, while they might privately laugh at the animal heads sported by members of the Egyptian pantheon, could easily accommodate them within their own beliefs.

Thus, Amun had already been identified with Zeus, the king of the Greek gods, before the Macedonian conquest. Other Egyptian divinities came to be associated with many members of the extensive Greek pantheon. Moreover, Ptolemy I consciously worked to pull together his Greek settlers and soldiers with the native Egyptian populace by uniting Egyptian and Greek deities. He consulted with a religious expert named Manethon, who advised him to adopt a new god – Serapis – as the patron of the dynasty. Serapis was a fusion of the Egyptian Osiris and Apis, but his worship incorporated Greek religious elements. Also, although the Ptolemies continued to worship the Greek gods, they were perfectly willing to perform rituals honouring the traditional gods on state occasions, and not only left the Egyptian priesthoods in place, but also patronized them.

To that extent at least, the Ptolemies were true Egyptian pharaohs, and one should not underestimate how important the performance of worship rituals was to the office of pharaoh. They were also content to maintain their control of the

ABOVE: Head of the god Serapis, depicted with his typical curling hair and beard.

kingdom through traditional political channels, although they introduced Greek financial institutions to assure a greater profit from their state. Nonetheless, the extent to which the Ptolemies 'went native' was strictly limited. The Ptolemies did not intermarry with Egypt's great noble families, and only the last member of the dynasty, Cleopatra VII, ever bothered to learn Egyptian. They operated a dual system, providing Greek law for Greeks while maintaining traditional law for their Egyptian subjects. Except for being crowned in Memphis as pharaohs (which probably all the Ptolemies did, although it is first attested with Ptolemy V), the members of the dynasty rarely ventured beyond Alexandria. And Alexandria, despite ancient monuments that were brought from the rest of Egypt to decorate its temples, was very much a Greek city.

The Ptolemies rarely ventured beyond Alexandria, which, despite ancient monuments that were brought from the rest of Egypt to decorate its temples, was very much a Greek city.

THE MIGHT OF ALEXANDRIA

Alexandria, Egypt, the greatest of the many cities Alexander founded (a number of which were also named Alexandria), flourished. By the mid-3rd century BC, its population had reached about 200,000, and by the early Roman period it had mounted to perhaps half a million. It became known as 'Alexandria *beside* Egypt', as if the city were a separate, independent country of its own. The Roman orator Dio of Prusa in the 1st century AD even described Egypt as an appendage of Alexandria rather than the other way around; it was probably a fair assessment from a political perspective. Alexandria became the great showplace of the Ptolemaic dynasty in their constant competition with the other Hellenistic kings. Two achievements stand out in particular, both initiated by the founder of the dynasty. Ptolemy I began construction of a massive lighthouse on Pharos Island at the mouth of Alexandria's main harbour. It is hard to imagine that such an elaborate edifice was really necessary to protect shipping. The structure, completed by Ptolemy II, stood 122m (400ft) tall; the light at the top could be seen 40km (25 miles) out to sea. The lower two of its three tiers were expensively faced with marble, while the

BELOW: An artist's reconstruction of what the great lighthouse of Alexandria might have looked like. Hailed as one of the seven wonders of the ancient world, the lighthouse's grandeur is typical of Ptolemaic showmanship.

ABOVE: **'Ptolemy I Soter Inaugurates the Great Library at Alexandria.' The 19th-century illustrator has constructed an exotically Egyptian scene, but in reality the museum and library the Ptolemies endowed was a thoroughly Greek institution.**

top was plastered, and an extensive statuary programme added to its aesthetic appeal. So strongly constructed that it was still mostly intact in the 12 century AD, the Lighthouse of Alexandria only met its end in 1477 when the remains of the building were used to construct a fortress.

Ptolemy I's other great showplace was the Mouseion, the temple of the Muses that became the centre of a large research institute and library. It was emphatically the home of *Greek* rather than Egyptian culture, created at the recommendation of the philosopher Demetrius of Phalerum. For centuries, the Ptolemies maintained resident and visiting scholars and invested heavily in an aggressive campaign of book acquisition for the Mouseion's great library. Within 200 years, the library contained about 700,000 papyrus manuscripts and was a magnet for learned people from throughout the Greek world. Unfortunately, the Mouseion and its library did not survive the tests of time either. It was partly burned in 48 BC and again when Zenobia of Palmyra attacked Alexandria in AD 270; most of the rest was destroyed when Caliph Omar occupied Alexandria in AD 642.

What most Egyptians beyond the boundaries of Alexandria would have seen of their monarchs was a hybrid rule. They used coins that looked like those of other Hellenistic states, but if an Egyptian visited a temple, they would have been confronted by the images of very traditional Egyptian pharaohs carved on the walls, their deeds proclaimed in hieroglyphs. Only a close look would reveal a slight Mediterranean influence in the shaping or pose of the ruler's body. Nonetheless, some images would have jarred. The Ptolemies (including some of their queens) often presented themselves in Greek military clothing, deploying a deliberate authoritarian symbol. We can only imagine what viewers made of the stele Ptolemy IV had erected recording the Raphia decree: Egypt's pharaoh was depicted in Macedonian armour astride a rearing horse, but also wearing the double crown of Egypt. We would know a great deal more about the dynasty if we had its tombs, but the Ptolemies chose to be buried in the Soma near Alexander the Great, so their final resting places have vanished along with his. Thus, despite the great deal of written material that has survived from this final dynasty (thanks to a new fashion in making cartonnage coffins, a process like papier mâché that involved enormous quantities of used papyrus), it is difficult to gauge how much the Ptolemies ever really adopted elements of Egyptian culture. We do know that they encouraged the study of Greek and sponsored Greek cultural events; teachers of Greek, athletes and actors were all exempt from the salt tax. Ordinary Egyptians also picked up a considerable quantity of the Greek language over time, as can be seen in Coptic, the lineal descendant of the Egyptian language.

Inasmuch as the early Ptolemies had an overarching policy, it was firmly directed towards dominance in the Hellenistic world. Alexander the Great's shadow was long, as were the wars of the Successors, as each of Alexander's generals struggled to keep Alexander's empire intact – under their own rule of course. Even before Alexander's dynasty ended with the murder of his son, the commanders were jostling each other for greater territory. Thus, Perdiccas invaded Egypt in 321 BC and Antigonus in 306 BC, but the future Ptolemy I was able to beat off both attacks. From the Ptolemaic perspective, it was not simply a matter of defending their new Egyptian kingdom from attack; they were also eager

BELOW: **Gold eight-drachma coin of Ptolemy IV Philopator, wearing the crown that became typical of Hellenistic monarchs. The trident is an allusion to his naval victories.**

The Ptolemies excelled at the Hellenistic game of showing off, flaunting their wealth.

to take possession of more lands, especially Syrian territories controlled by the Seleucids. No fewer than six Syrian Wars were fought from the reign of Ptolemy II (285–246 BC) to that of Ptolemy VI (180–145 BC), even though the matter was really settled when Egypt lost the Battle of Panion in 200 BC and soon gave up all claim to Syria and Phoenicia.

Nor was the war for power and influence limited to the battlefield. The Ptolemies excelled at the Hellenistic game of showing off, flaunting their wealth especially where the Greek world could see it and marvel. One example is the massive amount of aid Ptolemy III (246–221 BC) sent to Rhodes after the island suffered a devastating earthquake in 227 BC. The Ptolemies or their advisers were clever, however, and also made some effort to win friends in Egypt even while they fought their fellow Greeks. Alexander's expulsion of the Persians from Egypt was gradually equated to Ahmose's expulsion of the Hyksos, and the recovery of sacred statues the Persians had seized became a priority. The first four Ptolemies all reported recovering statues in the course of the Syrian Wars. Ptolemy II even held a great festival to celebrate their return, summoning priests from all over Egypt to join the festivities.

INCOME, INVESTMENT AND INFRASTRUCTURE

The rivalries of the Hellenistic world cost a great deal of money, but the rulers of Egypt were not only able to tap into the great resources that had always been available to the pharaohs but to generate new income streams. Ptolemy II Philadelphus (285–246 BC) was particularly successful in this regard. He is credited with some of the most efficient, punitive taxation in the world, his agents assuring that Egyptian commoners paid even more of their income into the royal treasury. Besides the Syrian Wars, he needed the money because he had to pay for the completion of his father's great enterprises in Alexandria, and the construction of great temples like that of Isis at Philae. The second Ptolemy also invested in projects designed to increase royal wealth in the long term. He restored the canal linking the Gulf of Suez and the eastern Delta, once again easing commerce not just along the eastern coast of Africa but with the Arabian Peninsula and beyond. Even more important, he restored the great hydraulic works the Middle Kingdom pharaohs had undertaken in the Faiyum, rebuilding or constructing from scratch the massive work of dykes and canals that perhaps tripled the amount of arable land in the Faiyum. It was Ptolemy II's efforts that made Egypt the breadbasket of the Mediterranean, the rich new farmland of the Faiyum region repeatedly

ABOVE: **Ptolemy II Philadelphus talking with Jewish scholars in the Library of Alexandria, by Jean Baptiste de Champaigne (1672). Ptolemy II commissioned the translation of Hebrew scripture into Greek known as the *Septuagint*.**

producing crops that were enormous by the standards of the day. Ptolemy II constructed a new town in the Faiyum to aid in its exploitation, and also established a port town at the terminal point of the canal. Both were named Arsinöe in honour of his sister-wife. Ptolemy II was probably the richest man in the world in his time.

TENSIONS RISE

The Ptolemaic Empire reached its greatest extent under Ptolemy III Euergetes I – since all male rulers of the dynasty were named Ptolemy, scholars usually employ their additional titles to distinguish them from each other. Ptolemy III's empire included Libya, northern Nubia and most of Syria. The king campaigned constantly, leaving his queen, Berenice, to serve as regent for five years during which he was absent in Asia. He also built extensively, establishing a sister city to Alexandria in Upper Egypt and beginning construction of the massive temple of Horus at Edfu. This Ptolemy was given (or took for himself) the title *euergetes*, which means 'benefactor', probably above all for his role in colonizing the Faiyum. But all was not well in Egypt, and his nod to traditional religion by starting the temple of Horus may have been intended to soothe political tensions. If that was the case, it did not work. Ptolemy III had imposed especially high taxes to finance his

POLITICAL DIVINITY

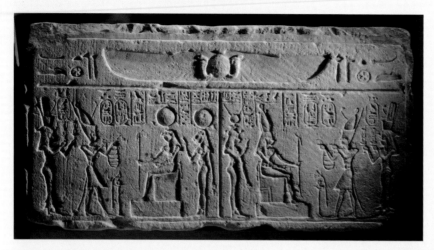

LEFT: **This limestone relief depicts Ptolemy II and Arsinöe II making offerings to the gods. Depicted in the age-old style of Egyptian royal portraiture, such works form a strong contrast to the Greek-style art the Ptolemies commissioned for themselves in Alexandria.**

Besides declaring Alexander the Great a god, like other Hellenistic rulers the Ptolemies declared that they too were divine. Posthumous veneration of a ruler was nothing new; it was in fact the norm for Egyptian pharaohs, so it probably raised few eyebrows when Ptolemy II deified his father Ptolemy I, ordaining a festival every four years in his honour. But Ptolemy II in 272 or 271 BC also deified himself and his sister-queen Arsinöe II, proclaiming their worship as 'brother–sister gods'. The inspiration for this act is to be found in the Greek world rather than Egypt, where similar proclamations of divinity for political ends had grown in popularity for several generations. Ptolemy II followed a typical Greek pattern by claiming descent from Herakles and Dionysus, as Macedonian kings before him had done. The increased ceremonial trappings associated with his claims of godhood probably gave greater force to the Greek pharaoh's edicts and served as a useful tool of government. The rest of the dynasty followed the same practice – for example, Ptolemy III (246–221 BC) and Berenice having themselves declared gods in 238 BC.

Part of the divine claim, which became standard with the later Ptolemies, was the practice that became standard of brother–sister marriage. It is unlikely that Egyptian tradition was the source for that Ptolemaic practice either. The marriage of full siblings was in fact rare in Egyptian history, and marriage even to half-siblings had become uncommon by the Third Intermediate and Late Periods. The Ptolemaic marriage practice was instead wrapped up with Greek notions of divinity, the rulers re-enacting the incestuous nuptials of the gods. In time, though, the Ptolemaic custom of sibling marriage must have had an unfortunate genetic effect. When the pharaohs of earlier dynasties had wed siblings, they had widened the gene pool by also taking other wives, sometimes many of them, making it very rare that full siblings would marry and likely that the heir to the throne would have royal blood only on the father's side. The Greeks, by contrast, were usually monogamous, so for generations at a time genetic weaknesses were passed down to heirs from both their parents.

wars, and the growing economic disparity between his Greek and Egyptian subjects created massive resentment. Nature also conspired against Ptolemy III; major flooding of the lower Nile in 245 BC devastated the harvest, and although the king imported grain to help his starving people, there was great hardship. Under such circumstances, it is hardly surprising that there was large-scale disaffection with the Greek pharaoh, marked by strikes, flight from settlements and brigandage. Ptolemy III saw the first of what became frequent native revolts, often launched in the hope of displacing the Ptolemies and restoring native rule.

Tensions continued to rise in the reign of Ptolemy IV Philopater (221–205 BC). He embroiled Egypt in the monstrously expensive Fourth Syrian War. The pharaoh won a major victory over the Seleucid Antiochus III in 217 BC in the Battle of Raphia, thanks especially to the use of heavier African war elephants against Antiochus' Indian ones. But Egypt's military build-up had shifted the balance of Ptolemaic control. Since the Macedonian soldier class in Egypt over time became a small minority, Ptolemy IV had recourse to native Egyptian troops who were trained to fight using Macedonian tactics, equipping them as heavy infantrymen and employing the Macedonian phalanx. The Egyptian soldiers did well at Raphia, but rioted upon their return to Egypt, finding the preferential treatment accorded to Greek fighters

ABOVE: The main entrance of the temple of Horus at Edfu. Constructed by order of the Ptolemies (perhaps replacing an earlier temple on the same site), the structure is one of the best-preserved temples of ancient Egypt.

intolerable. Ptolemy was forced to begin allotting land to Egyptian soldiers as the Ptolemies always had to Greeks, although the natives received smaller, poorer plots of land. Those 20,000 Egyptian fighting men would have seen the extravagance of the court and brought back reports to their own poor villages.

Ptolemy IV was deeply unpopular, thanks not just to his high taxes and unequal treatment of natives but also to his personally dissolute lifestyle. Very much manipulated by favourites, especially his chief adviser Sosibius, Ptolemy enriched his courtiers but did not hesitate even to have his own brother Magas scalded to death in response to a rumour that Ptolemy had poisoned their mother, Berenice. A native rebellion broke out towards the end of Ptolemy IV's reign, starting in the Delta but soon spreading nationwide.

The result was the Great Revolt of 206–186 BC. Unrest was quickly put down in the Delta, but not before it had spread to Upper Egypt. The rebellion based on Thebes proved to be a much more serious matter. Its leader, an Egyptian noble named Herwennefer, declared himself pharaoh and tried to form an independent state of Upper Egypt. Although Herwennefer died in 200 BC, his successor Ankhwennefer continued the struggle until 186 BC. Although some modern scholars have seen the hand of the high priest of Amun in Thebes behind the rebellion, the revolt does not seem to have been against foreign rule per se, but rather was a reaction to badly declining living standards. The two would-be pharaohs succeeded in ruling much of the Nile Valley for nearly two decades, receiving aid from Nubia in their bid for independence.

DYNASTIC STRIFE

The rebel 'dynasty' lasted as long as it did because of chaos at the heart of Ptolemaic government. Ptolemy IV died in 205 BC, leaving the throne to the five-year-old Ptolemy V Epiphanes (205–180 BC). But for several years there was no clear head of the government for the child pharaoh. Ptolemy IV's mistress Agathoclea had joined with her brother Agathocles to murder the queen mother Arsinöe and seize the regency for themselves. The governor of Pelusium eventually marched his army on Alexandria to avenge the queen, joined on the way by Egyptian villagers and reinforced in the capital by an Alexandrian mob. That mob then broke into the royal palace in Alexandria and beat Agathocles and his family to death. A number of other regents followed before Ptolemy V, by then 12 years old, was crowned at Memphis, the ceremony perhaps deliberately timed in an effort to calm the civil strife that was still rocking Egypt. We know about that coronation thanks to the Rosetta Stone, the famous trilingual inscription that was the key to the decipherment of hieroglyphs. Inscribed in 196 BC, the stone preserves a decree by the

OPPOSITE: **Painted and gilded stela of Ptolemy V Epiphanes making an offering to the Buchis bull. The Buchis bull was held to be a manifestation of the god Ptah. The Buchis and Apis bulls are only two of the many animal cults of late pharaonic Egypt.**

priests of Memphis, reporting the young king's coronation and the re-establishment of Ptolemaic rule over Egypt. Nonetheless, it took years to bring the rebellion to an end. The process disrupted the economy of Upper Egypt for 20 years, as the Ptolemaic campaigns against the rebels devastated a large number of villages. Two other Hellenistic rulers, the Antigonid king Philip V and the Seleucid Antiochus III, also took advantage of Egypt's disorder to seize territory in the Fifth Syrian War, in which the Ptolemies lost their territories in western Asia and most of their power in the eastern Mediterranean.

The Ptolemies survived, but their power was deeply eroded. Ptolemy V eventually made peace with the Seleucids, marrying Antiochus III's daughter Cleopatra to seal the new alliance. It is probably during his reign that the city of Ptolemais was developed as a second administrative centre in the south. It served as a counterweight to Thebes, still largely controlled by the priests of Amun. New long-term military camps were also established in the Thebaid, sometimes using temple enclosures, for example at Rameses III's great temple at Medinet Habu. The later Ptolemies also gradually introduced more Greek offices, gradually displacing the Egyptian aristocracy from the administrative posts that many families had held without interruption for centuries. Ptolemy V marked his regaining of control in Upper Egypt with construction projects, including the great temple project at Philae, which had to be moved to keep it from being submerged when the Aswan High Dam was completed.

The Greek historian Polybius blames the decline of the Ptolemaic dynasty on the unsatisfactory character of Ptolemy IV, but the reality was larger than that. Repeated dynastic strife rocked the monarchy from the childhood of Ptolemy V on, a situation repeatedly exacerbated by unruly Alexandrian mobs. Whether from failure of will, incompetence or simply because they were too busy combatting other threats, the late Ptolemies allowed discord to spread with little check. What was at issue was not pro-Egyptian nationalism, with patriots taking arms against foreign rulers. Rather, the increasingly weak monarchy allowed ancient rivalries to resurface, as when Crocodilopolis went to war with its neighbouring rival in the reign of Ptolemy VIII.

ABOVE: **The Rosetta Stone. Discovered by French soldiers campaigning in Egypt in 1799, the stone is inscribed with a decree issued in 196 BC in hieroglyphic and demotic script as well as Greek. It was the key to the decipherment of ancient Egyptian.**

Repeated dynastic strife rocked the monarchy. The late Ptolemies allowed discord to spread with little check.

Engraved for
Middleton's Complete
System of Geography.

The Interview of the Roman Ambassador
POPILLIUS, with KING ANTIOCHUS in Egypt.

LEFT: This 1779 engraving shows the sublimely arrogant Roman envoy Gaius Popillius Laenas issuing his famous ultimatum to Antiochus IV Epiphanes, forcing the latter to withdraw from Egypt.

OVERLEAF: Ptolemy VI Philometor paying homage to the deity Sobek. Although carried out in traditional Egyptian style, the more curved figures with more highly defined muscles demonstrate the influence of Greek art.

And then there was Rome. By the 2nd century BC, the Roman Republic had developed into the first great superpower of the western Mediterranean, and started intervening in affairs to the east, often with the encouragement of Hellenistic rulers who wanted to hold up Rome as a threat against their enemies. Nowhere was this more obvious than in Egypt. In 168 BC, Antiochus IV encroached on Ptolemaic territory. It would not have suited Rome, however, for the Seleucids to add wealthy Egypt to their own empire. So, the Senate dispatched Gaius Popillius Laenas to order Antiochus to cease and desist. They met outside Alexandria. With consummate Roman arrogance, Laenas drew a circle in the sand around the king and demanded Antiochus' answer before he stepped over the line. Antiochus left Egypt and Ptolemaic control of Egypt was preserved, but only at the cost of growing dependence on Rome.

After the reign of Ptolemy V, the history of the dynasty becomes a confused web of rivalries and weak rulers. Ptolemy VI Philometor (180–145 BC) inherited the throne at the age of six. A series of regents controlled Egypt during his minority, including after 170 BC the pharaoh's elder sister (and wife) Cleopatra II. Although the Romans had driven the Seleucids away from Egypt's borders in 168 BC, that did not end the threat. Egypt suffered major defeats in the Sixth Syrian War, which gave Philometor's younger brother, confusingly known as Ptolemy VIII (Ptolemy VI's son, the seventh of the name, ruled briefly in 145 BC), the opportunity to expel the king and seize the throne for himself. Ptolemy VIII Euergetes held on to the throne for a number of years. He roused so much resentment in Alexandria, however, with measures that included marriage both to his sister Cleopatra II (despite the fact that she was already wed to Ptolemy VI) and his niece Cleopatra III (they were known as 'Cleopatra the Sister' and 'Cleopatra the Wife') that the Alexandrians invited Ptolemy VI back to the throne in 163 BC. The restored king proved to be considerably more successful in his second reign. He won a complete victory over the Seleucids at the Battle of the Oenoparus in 145 BC and assumed rule of his great Hellenistic rival. Ptolemy VI only had three days to savour his triumph, however, before dying of his battle wounds, and Ptolemaic control of Syria was almost immediately lost again.

BELOW: **Diorite head of Ptolemy VIII Euergetes II. The artist has caught some of the physical characteristics of Ptolemy, who was nicknamed 'Physcon', 'the balloon', because of his obesity.**

Legend tells us that the vengeful Ptolemy VIII killed his own son by the rebellious wife, Cleopatra II, then sent the boy's dismembered body to her as a birthday present.

The exiled brother, Ptolemy VIII Euergetes, soon returned to Egypt, deposing and executing Ptolemy VI's son and heir; he ruled until his death in 116 BC. His second reign was far from peaceful, however, as his wives joined court factions. Cleopatra II led a rebellion against Ptolemy VIII in *c.*132 BC, driving him and his other wife out of Alexandria. Legend tells that the vengeful king killed his own son by the rebellious wife, then sent the boy's dismembered body to Cleopatra II as a birthday present. A short burst of native rebellion sought to take advantage of the civil war within the Greek ruling class. In 131 BC, a man named Harsiese claimed the royal title for a short time in Thebes, but was soon driven out. The most interesting points about this rebellion were that, as so often before, Thebes was the focal point of discontent, and that it was accompanied by political prophecy. A self-

BELOW: **Head of Cleopatra II, originally part of a larger basalt statue. The art of ancient Egypt is scattered around the world; this example now resides in the Kunsthistorisches Museum of Vienna.**

proclaimed prophet known only as 'The Potter' announced the return of the 'Great Spirit' (by which he probably meant *maat*, the force of order of which the pharaohs were the guardians) to Memphis. Evil would end, the foreigners would drop dead and Alexandria would be reduced to a fishing village. Such a prophecy certainly demonstrates that the native Egyptians' woes were not simply economic.

Ptolemy VIII and Cleopatra were rather surprisingly reconciled eventually, and they ruled jointly until Ptolemy's death. Cleopatra II apparently died soon afterwards, and Cleopatra III became co-ruler with *her* son Ptolemy IX. The queen mother proved unwilling to share power with the boy. In 106 BC, Ptolemy IX was accused of plotting against her. That it was he rather than she who was forced to flee the country demonstrates well that it was Cleopatra III who was the real power on the throne. In her elder son's place, Cleopatra installed her younger son as

Ptolemy X (107–88 BC), marrying him to consolidate their joint hold on the throne and make sure her influence did not wane. He may have arranged his mother's death in 101 BC; if he did, it may have been in self-defence when he received reports that she was intending to kill him.

ABOVE: **Relief of Ptolemy VIII Euergetes II with his two wives Cleopatra II and Cleopatra III, from the temple of Sobek and Haroeris in Kom Ombo.**

The panorama of the late Ptolemies is not very edifying. Ptolemy X married his niece Berenice III and continued the Hellenistic trend of investing real power in the queen by elevating her to the position of co-ruler. Nonetheless, much of the tenth Ptolemy's reign was spent trying to thwart his brother's efforts to return. Yet another Theban rebellion, which broke out in 91 or 90 BC, and the embattled ruler lost control of the south. As if that weren't enough to contend with, the Alexandrians and army soon turned against Ptolemy X as well and expelled him. According to Porphyry, this was because the king was too friendly with the large Jewish populace of Alexandria, who lived in a state of considerable tension with the Greeks there; Strabo, however, says the king raised the mob's anger by melting down Alexander the Great's golden sarcophagus to raise funds for war. Whichever the case, the Alexandrians invited Ptolemy IX to return, which he did. Ptolemy X and Berenice tried twice to stage a come-back, but on their second invasion of Cyprus the exiled king was killed.

The civil war drained Egypt's treasury, and Ptolemy borrowed a great deal of money from Rome to fight his brother. It was probably reason, rather

than simple hatred of the people who had exiled him, that led Ptolemy X to leave Egypt itself to Rome in his will. The Romans chose not to take possession, but thanks to debt and that rash promise, the threat of Roman intervention in Egypt loomed ever closer. Indeed, one by one, Rome was defeating the other Hellenistic kingdoms. Egypt was the plum of the collection, enjoying fabled wealth and already exporting large quantities of grain to Rome every year. For the time being, Rome was content to maintain the Ptolemaic kings in a state of clientage, probably mostly because of fear that the conquest of Egypt would raise a single Roman general to such prominence that the Senate would be unable to contain him.

The rivalry between the ninth and tenth Ptolemies continued at the start of the next reign, in 80 BC. Ptolemy IX did not produce a legitimate son, so upon his death his daughter Berenice III, who had also been the wife of her uncle Ptolemy X, inherited the throne. She then married Ptolemy X's son by another wife; the youthful Ptolemy XI was her stepson and cousin. However, only a few days into their joint reign, Ptolemy XI murdered Berenice. He had not reckoned with her great popularity in Alexandria, and an Alexandrian mob soon lynched him. After the familial bloodbaths, almost the last remaining member of the dynasty was an illegitimate son of Ptolemy IX, who was recalled to Egypt and proclaimed as Ptolemy XII Neos Dionysos (more commonly mockingly called Auletes, the 'flute player') (80–51 BC).

The flute player's reign was a constant juggling act as he tried to balance the threat of Rome against the peril of internal dissent. The power-hungry men vying for power in Rome realized they could extract money from

LEFT: Relief showing the gods Horus, Thoth and Haroeris purifying Ptolemy XII Neos Dionysos, more popularly known as 'the Fluteplayer', from Kom Ombo.

Cleopatra was an astute ruler, fighting desperately to preserve her dynasty by any means available to her, including sexual favours.

Auletes with the threat of foreclosing on Rome's loans or throwing their support to a rival claimant for the Egyptian throne. As a result, Ptolemy XII had little choice but to bankroll Pompey the Great's campaigns in the east, even though he had to raise taxes and cut back on administrative costs to do so. His exactions caused a final native revolt against the Ptolemies, which was suppressed with considerable brutality.

Trying to improve his circumstances within his kingdom, Ptolemy borrowed heavily from Roman moneylenders. Finally, in 60 BC, he achieved a diplomatic coup when Rome recognized Egypt as a formal friend and ally – the best possible protection against invasion by Rome or anyone else. But the price was high. Ptolemy only accomplished Rome's recognition by means of a massive bribe offered to the two leading Romans, Pompey and Julius Caesar, an amount that apparently equalled the entire annual revenue of the Egyptian monarchy. Even that did not save Auletes from a coup by his own daughter, Berenice IV, who was left in Egypt as regent in 58 BC when the king went to Rome and successfully blocked her father's return for three years. Ptolemy was only able to re-establish himself with Roman military aid, and executed his unfilial daughter.

BELOW: **The Battle of Pharsalus and the Death of Pompey, produced by the workshop of the Florentine Apollonio di Giovanni di Tomaso and his successor Marco del Buono Giamberti (1455/1460).**

CLEOPATRA, JULIUS CAESAR AND MARK ANTONY

When Ptolemy XII died in 51 BC, he left the throne jointly to his remaining daughter Cleopatra VII Philopator and her younger brother Ptolemy XIII. The bloody struggle for control of Egypt continued, though, as Ptolemy XIII grew up and he (or the eunuch Pothinus who served as Ptolomy's chief adviser) resented his sister's hold on power. They forced Cleopatra to flee to Syria, but she raised an army and soon returned to wage a civil war against her brother.

And then Rome appeared on the scene. Julius Caesar had decisively defeated his rival Pompey and Pompey fled for refuge to Egypt. The young Ptolemy XIII, thinking it would please the victor, had Pompey killed and presented his head to Caesar when Caesar arrived in pursuit of his enemy. The disgusted Caesar then threw his support behind Cleopatra, and found his small force besieged in Alexandria for months, under attack by the army of Ptolemy XIII and his youngest sister Arsinöe. When Roman reinforcements arrived, Caesar took the offensive and defeated Ptolemy in the Battle of the Nile at the beginning of 47 BC. The 15-year-old Ptolemy XIII was drowned in the river.

Cleopatra named her younger brother Ptolemy XIV as co-ruler, although in fact she governed the state and barely even acknowledged her new brother-husband. Much more important was Cleopatra VII's affair with Julius Caesar, which produced a son commonly known as Caesarion, who took the name Ptolemy XV and shared rule with his mother after Ptolemy XIV died in 44 BC.

OVERLEAF: **'Caesar meeting Cleopatra', by Giovanni Domenico Tiepolo (1747).**

Cleopatra was an astute ruler, fighting desperately to preserve her dynasty by any means available to her, including sexual favours. She was in most ways a typical Hellenistic queen, paying lip service to the traditions of Egypt but in Alexandria living and representing herself very much as a Greek. She did, however, take the unusual step – the only member of her dynasty to do so – of learning Egyptian, along with at least six other languages. According to traditional accounts, she was not classically beautiful, but her charm and vivacity beguiled those around her.

Cleopatra was in Rome in 44 BC when Julius Caesar was assassinated. She fled back to Egypt and had her son Caesarion acclaimed as co-ruler (it's possible that she had Ptolemy XIV poisoned to create the vacancy on the throne). Her position was not tenable as Rome moved yet again towards civil war. The greatest threat was from Julius Caesar's legal heir, his great-nephew Octavian, who naturally resented the very existence of Caesar's son Caesarion, even though he was illegitimate by Roman standards. As a counterweight to Octavian's belligerence, Cleopatra formed a new alliance in every sense of the word with his chief rival, Caesar's lieutenant Mark Antony. Egyptian queen and Roman triumvir married, Antony divorcing his Roman wife – Octavian's sister – to do so, and the couple produced two children.

War was, however, inevitable between Mark Antony and Octavian, and Cleopatra was forced by her relationship with Antony into the conflict. Antony and Cleopatra's navy was decisively defeated in the Battle of Actium in September 31 BC. They fled back to Egypt, but were unable to muster a sufficient defence against the pursuing Octavian. Mark Antony committed suicide and, although she hoped for a time to make a deal that would preserve her throne, Cleopatra VII followed suit on 10 August 30 BC. When Octavian took control of Egypt, the last pharaoh, Ptolemy XV Caesarion, was killed as well.

THE END OF AN ERA

The death of Cleopatra VII and her son Caesarion marks the end of pharaonic Egypt and the demise of Egypt as an independent state. Egypt became just another province of Rome, although one so wealthy that Octavian, or Augustus Caesar as he soon came to be called, kept it under his personal control. Augustus and his successors were not, however, pharaohs. Augustus marked his attitude towards Egyptian culture by refusing to honour the Apis bull or the mummies of the ancient kings. What concerned him instead was the fiscal efficiency of his new province; he toured the Nile Valley and ordered repairs to the irrigation system. In general, Augustus and his successors appear to have felt little but contempt for the Egyptian people, regarding

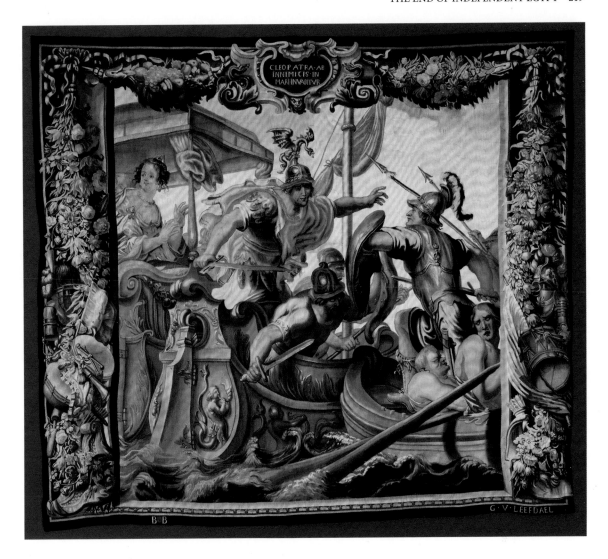

them as fanatical, superstitious, ignorant and prone to rebellion. Unlike other provincials, Augustus did not even employ Egyptians in the administration of his empire, excluding them from the Senate and even from the army. The administration within Egypt itself was left mostly in the hands of Greeks. The Roman emperors rarely visited Egypt and were not crowned, nor did they present themselves as the guardians of *maat*.

Egypt without a pharaoh was unimaginable, so Egyptian priests simply bestowed traditional royal titles on the Roman emperors and depicted them in the temples as traditional kings; it is doubtful that the emperors themselves were even aware that they were being presented in that way. Especially with the coming of Christianity, the memory of the 3,000-year-long history of the pharaohs gradually faded away, and was only recovered by the archaeologists of the 19th and 20th centuries.

SUGGESTIONS FOR FURTHER READING

PRIMARY SOURCES

Lichtheim, Miriam, ed. *Ancient Egyptian Literature*. Berkeley: University of California Press, 1973.

Manetho. *History of Egypt and Other Works*. Translated by W.G. Waddell. Cambridge: Harvard University Press, 1940.

Moran, William L., ed. and trans. *The Amarna Letters*. Baltimore: Johns Hopkins University Press, 1992.

Parkinson, R.B., trans. *The Tale of Sinuhe and Other Ancient Egyptian Poems, 1940–1640 BC*. Oxford: Oxford University Press, 1997.

STUDIES

Bárta, Miroslav. *Analyzing Collapse: The Rise and Fall of the Old Kingdom*. American University in Cairo Press, 2019.

Barwik, Miroslaw. *The Twilight of Ramesside Egypt*. Warsaw: Agade, 2011.

Bédoyère, Guy de la. *Pharaohs of the Sun*. New York: Pegasus, 2023.

Bestock, Laurel. *Violence and Power in Ancient Egypt*. London: Routledge, 2017.

Booth, Charlotte. *Horemheb: The Forgotten Pharaoh*. Stroud: Amberley, 2009.

Bowman, Alan. *Egypt after the Pharaohs, 332 BC–AD 642*. Berkeley: University of California Press, 1996.

Chauveau, Michel. *Egypt in the Age of Cleopatra*. Ithaca, NY: Cornell University Press, 1997.

Cline, E.H. *1177 BC: The Year Civilization Collapsed*. Princeton, NJ: Princeton University Press, 2014.

Cline, E.H., and D. O'Connor, eds. *Ramesses III: The Life and Times of Egypt's Last Hero*. Ann Arbor: University of Michigan Press, 2012.

Creasman, Pearce Paul, and Richard H. Wilkinson, eds. *Pharaoh's Land and Beyond: Ancient Egypt and Its Neighbors*. Oxford: Oxford University Press, 2017.

Dodson, Aidan. *The Pyramids of Ancient Egypt*. London: New Holland, 2003.

Fagan, Brian. *The Rape of the Nile: Tomb Robbers, Tourists, and Archaeologists in Egypt*. Rev. ed. London: Basic Books, 2004.

Gardiner, A.H. *Egypt of the Pharaohs*. 3rd ed. Oxford: Oxford University Press, 2006.

Grajetzki, Wolfram. *The Middle Kingdom of Ancient Egypt*. London: Duckworth, 2006.

Hawass, Zahi, and Sahar N. Saleem. *Scanning the Pharaohs*. Cairo: American University in Cairo Press, 2016.

Hölbl, Günther. *A History of the Ptolemaic Empire*. Translated by Tina Saavedra. London: Routledge, 2001.

Kitchen, K.A. *The Third Intermediate Period in Egypt*. 2nd ed. Warminster: Aris and Phillips, 1995.

Lehner, M., and Z. Hawass. *Giza and the Pyramids: The Definitive History*. Chicago: University of Chicago Press, 2017.

Morris, Ellen. *Ancient Egyptian Imperialism*. Hoboken, NJ: Wiley, 2018.

Mourad, A.-L. *Rise of the Hyksos: Egypt and the Levant from the Middle Kingdom to the Early Second Intermediate Period*. Oxford: Archaeopress, 2015.

Myśliwiec, Karol. *The Twilight of Ancient Egypt: First Millennium B.C.E.*. Translated by David Lorton. Ithaca, NY: Cornel University Press, 2000.

Roehrig, C.R., ed. *Hatshepsut: From Queen to Pharaoh*. New York: Metropolitan Museum of Art, 2005.

Ryan, Donald P. *Ancient Egypt: The Basics*. London: Routledge, 2016.

Sabbahy, Lisa K. *Kingship, Power, and Legitimacy in Ancient Egypt: From the Old Kingdom to the Middle Kingdom*. Cambridge: Cambridge University Press, 2020.

Shaw, Ian, ed. *The Oxford History of Ancient Egypt*. 2nd ed. Oxford: Oxford University Press, 2003.

Teeter, Emily. *The Presentation of Maat: Ritual and Legitimacy in Ancient Egypt*. Chicago: Oriental Institute, 1997.

Tyldesley, Joyce. *Hatchepsut: The Female Pharaoh*. London: Penguin, 1998.

———. *Nefertiti: Egypt's Sun Queen*. London: Viking, 1998.

———. *The Pharaohs*. London: Quercus, 2009.

———. *The Private Lives of the Pharaohs*. New York: TV Books, 2001.

———. *Ramesses: Egypt's Greatest Pharaoh*. London: Penguin, 2000.

Wilkinson, Toby, A.H. *Early Dynastic Egypt*. London: Routledge, 1999.

INDEX

Picture credits

G